CW00732850

Reclaim Your Inner Goddess

7 Steps to Unlocking Your Inner Goddess Through
the Power of the Chakras

Stel Coombe-Heath

Ingrid Galloway

Eli Huang

Beth Dovey

Margie McCumstie

Shari Ware

Linda Joy Benn

ISBN: 978-0-6485048-2-5

Resources

To access the resources mentioned in this book go to
https://reclaimyourinnergoddess.com.au/resources

Kind Words

"I love this book awakening the sacred body has never felt so good. Finally a practical guide to fall in love with myself and my life. A must read for any woman who wants to - recenter yourself and reclaim your sacred empowerment. Ladies, join the revolution. It is time to reclaim your inner goddess!"

- Jemimah Ashleigh, The Visibility Lab
International Keynote Speaker
Best-selling Author

"Reclaim Your Inner Goddess is a practical, information rich guide written by seven enlightened authors, who share their life journeys and their own life struggles along the way to unblock the relevant chakra that they identified as holding them back or sabotaging their success. What I particularly liked was the practical format of listing a stack of symptoms or behaviours for the reader to identify as patterns of their own self-sabotage. This was followed by a variety of tools that the reader could use to address that behaviour, create daily habits and rituals to reclaim their inner goddess. This easy-to-understand format is a must for those just beginning to understand their chakra journeys as well as the spiritually minded reader who is aware of the power and benefit of unblocking and tapping into their chakras and what each chakra represents."

- Robyn Henderson, Networking Strategist

"As the proverb states: "when the student is ready, the teacher will appear!" This powerful collaboration will ignite the goodness within you so that you can live an empowered and vibrant life. Each of these heart centered authors/ teachers takes the reader on a journey into their own power. Well done ladies! Great read."

- Aeriol Ascher, Intuitive healing guide and empowerment leader
www.aeriolascher.com

"As the CEO and founder of Thriving Women in Business I understand the struggles women experience. In this book 'Reclaim your inner goddess ' you will learn several important tips which you can implement immediately to feel empowered, balanced, energized and in touch with my femininity to achieve the results you desire. My work is all about, positivity, integrity, generosity, community, and providing massive value while uplifting others. This book delivers all of that and more."

- Caterina Rando is a master certified coach, business strategist, speaker and author. Founder of the Thriving Women in Business Center, located in San Francisco.

"The seven authors have both alignment and specialisation. They each shared intimate personal stories about their life journey which made the advice they provided even more meaningful. I will purchase the hard copy to share it with others. I'll be using the resources too. Many thanks for writing and sharing your wisdom."

- Wendy Lloyd Curley, Founder of Strategic Networking

Contents

Foreword

Your inner goddess is powerful

She is confident – even when inwardly she might not be feeling that confidence

She has a glow – a glow that is alluring, is magnetic and she is at peace with who she truly is

Revealing your inner goddess means you have listened to your self-talk (maybe shut down the unhelpful words that don't serve you). You have courageously chosen to step into your power and be true to your authentic self. The authentic self that existed before the experiences of life left its imprint.

Unleashing and discovering your inner goddess means you have found your calling – you may have also taken the decision to share your knowledge, experience and passion with the world.

To these 7 remarkable women who have chosen to share their power and their stories – congratulations! They understand their message will create a better universe and it will resonate with the people that need to hear that message at the exact right time in the right way.

Congratulations for your bravery, your passion and your collective visions. The vulnerability and honesty of your own stories is both compelling and remarkable

Thank you for sharing your collective lived experiences and to develop teachings that will empower, educate and create change for the future inner goddesses of our world

To the prospective inner goddess, about to embark on your journey of discovery, I trust you will enjoy this wonderful tribute and handbook on how to reclaim your inner goddess as much as I did. There is a wealth of knowledge, reflection and practical advice to dive into

It's truly an honour to be asked to add to this collection of chapters that will continue to empower women of all ages for years to come.

I had the privilege of bringing these 7 women together through – to me the synergies they share is crystal clear and the possibilities were infinite. To see the vision I had for them come to fruition and for them to create this Inner Goddess handbook is uplifting and inspiring.

I trust you will open your heart and mind to approach your own expedition with the curiosity, openness and acceptance your future inner goddess deserves.

Enjoy the journey xxx
Laurene McKenzie
(aka Loz – Super Connector)

Welcome to the Adventure!

"The goddess doesn't enter us from outside; she emerges from deep within. She is not held back by what happened in the past. She is conceived in consciousness, born in love, and nurtured by higher thinking. She is integrity and value, created and sustained by the hard work of personal growth and the discipline of a life lived actively in hope."
– Marianne Williamson

Welcome to this book. Whether you bought it for yourself, was gifted it by a loved one or discovered it by some other means, it is meant to be in your hands now. There is a zen proverb that states "When the student is ready, the teacher will appear". Sometimes people ask for or look for a sign or a guidepost for their journey. This is it. Your higher self is the teacher, but this book will help guide you and lead you lovingly to yourself.

Just as it is no mistake that you are reading this book, it is also no mistake that it is titled "Reclaim your Inner Goddess". Let's look at the most important word in the title- Reclaim.

Firstly, to reclaim assumes that you once had an inner goddess. Even if you feel like this has never been the case for you personally or if the concept of being a goddess is foreign, the idea of reclaiming still assumes the inner goddess is within you.

Secondly, the patriarchal society in which we live has worked hard to push down, squeeze out and destroy the power of women over thousands of years. Strong, powerful women have been seen as a threat for a long time. Obedience and subservience to men has been held up as an ideal long before the 1950's. Witches have been burned, women have been shunned and our power as women has been denied. Our feminist sisters before us have laid foundations upon which we must continue to build with strength, resilience and courage. Which brings me to our third and most important reason that we used the word "reclaim".

Thirdly, to "reclaim" is not a passive step. This book can encourage, help you make revelations within yourself and guide you- but ultimately, it is YOU, dear reader, who must have the courage to reclaim your inner goddess. Before each chapter in this book, you will find a powerful quote. If you have a journal, why not write the quote out and let the words speak to your soul? This chapter is no different, so let us revisit the quote again. The fabulous Marianne Williamson once said "The Goddess doesn't enter us from outside; she emerges from deep within. She is not held back by what happened in the past. She is conceived in consciousness, born in love, and nurtured by higher thinking. She is integrity and value, created and sustained by the hard work of personal growth and the discipline of a life lived actively in hope." Our hope is that this book may create a stirring within you to allow your inner goddess to emerge and shine. We have our collective histories and our personal traumas and yet, if we are prepared to actively, lovingly and compassionately reclaim our inner goddess, we can be the powerful women we deserve to be. If we can step into our power courageously, reclaiming our inner goddess, we can be the powerful women that our families, our communities and our world deserves. It is time. It. Is. Time.

And so, here we are. Eight powerful women gathered together to whisper secrets, speak our guidance and sing of love. Our words are before you, ready to dance with your soul and help your inner goddess emerge to play with ours. There are seven main chakras and each of us wrote with a chakra in mind. "But hang on, you said eight women, not seven?" Ah yes, for you see the eighth woman gathered here is you. This book comes alive with your participation. As we share our truth, our wisdom and our love with vulnerability and passion, you are invited to draw towards you whatever you need to reclaim your inner goddess!

So, let me introduce you to my fellow contributors and you'll get to know them more through their unique voices and stories in each chapter and chakra.

Stel Coombe-Heath is the #1 authority in helping busy women stop binge eating. She is on a mission to help a million women have a better relationship with food and their body. Stel struggled with a disordered relationship with food and her body for over 13 years, battling two eating disorders, body dysmorphia and emotional eating. She is now passionate about a future where women and young girls are no longer ashamed of their bodies. Stel launches our journey through the chakras by commencing with the Root Chakra. Stel is a compassionate and resilient woman with an important message to share.

Our journey then continues with the Sacral Chakra. Ingrid Galloway is the Founder, Relationship Coach and Chief Relaxation Officer of Kahyangan®, which means "heaven". She has been a Relationship Coach since 2009 and a Spa Therapist since 1999. She practices from Kahyangan® in Sydney and from clients' homes, offices and hotel rooms, Online and from retreat locations! Her work has always focused on stress, relaxation and relationships. Ingrid is always ready to look after stressed people and the loving and not-so-loving couples. She does 1-1 coaching sessions, group online couples massage lessons, and retreats. Ingrid shares her story with vulnerability and an eagerness to connect.

We then move to the Solar Plexus Chakra and we are guided through by Eli Huang who has been a Beauty Therapist and Natural Health Practitioner for over 20 years. Eli's passion has always been in ageing and what you can do to look younger and feel healthier. Eli's studies have centred on discovering why someone ages more quickly than others and to discover the secrets of those who look youthful and live long, healthy, happy lives. Over the years, Eli has studied the science of ageing and how to slow down or even reverse ageing so we are years or decades younger than our biological age. Eli's vivacious nature and quest for knowledge make this a content rich chapter.

Then to the heart of the matter, the Heart Chakra with Beth Dovey. Beth is a Stress Recovery Specialist and coaches professionals away from stress, emotional reactivity, and feeling like they always have to have it all together. This allows them to step into their authenticity, aliveness and alignment with what is really important to them, so they live a life with no regrets. Beth combines the gold from 15 years of medical science with Metadynamics TM, positive psychology, coaching methodologies and emotional intelligence, along with her life experience. Beth is a warm, friendly woman with powerful insights to share.

My chapter is next and we delve into the Throat Chakra. My name is Margie McCumstie and I'm an acclaimed Speaker, Author and Entrepreneur with a mission to empower people to live courageous, inspired lives and for businesses to acknowledge and harness the gifts of their teams. I hope my words serve to catalyse positive transformation and personal growth, as well as human and business development. I'm also the founder and business owner of both Metamorphis Ceremonies and Love Legacy and my first book- "BeLoved- Remembering, Discovering and Creating who YOU are as you Journey through Life" was not only an Amazon bestseller, but continues to help raise funds for a number of charities. I'm proud to be a previous Winner of the Australian Small Business Champion Awards and the 2021 Altitude Awards Purpose Driven Award and share from a wealth of experience in business and life. I hope my chapter impacts your life with my words, empathy and resilience.

Above the throat, is the Third Eye Chakra and we continue our adventure with the fabulous Shari Ware. Shari is a Health Mindset Specialist, best selling author and international speaker who, after releasing 100kg naturally, is on a mission to help you to LEAP off the weight merry-go-round and navigate the path to a healthier you that's not defined by a number on a scale or the size of your body - she helps you to find YOUR healthy, YOUR way! Shari's insightful exploration of the Third Eye opens new possibilities with her fresh perspective.

And finally, we adjust our goddess crowns with Linda Joy Benn as together, we visit the Crown Chakra. Linda Joy is a transformational catalyst, international speaker and best-selling author. She's a spiritual mentor, coach and therapist with over 20 years of experience in the field of energy healing. Linda has developed ways of channeling the energies. She works with ascended masters to help people find their way to wholeness.

She has healed herself of cancer and autoimmune disease without medication. Also, transformed thousands of people's minds and bodies through her intuitive holistic approach.

As the founder of the Benn Method and 5R program, Linda identifies the root cause of blocked energy. To release it in the body and mind, she brings the life-force energy to that area. This results in miraculous healing and transformation. Whilst Linda is proud of her many awards and business successes in both the United States and Australia, it is the results she has achieved for her clients that brings her the greatest joy.

After years meeting and working with celebrities, she researched the secrets to their true success. This includes interviewing Dr Phil. They both share the same philosophy on the mind/body connection. Linda is on a mission to empower professionals to "take back control", connecting their head and heart. Linda is passionate about individuals being in alignment with their true authentic selves. Linda brings her strength and power to the Crown Chakra to help bring us into alignment to reconnect with our higher self.

The eighth valuable participant is you. By reading and interacting with our words, listening to our bonus materials, connecting with our Facebook community or joining in our live events, you are taking active steps to reclaim your inner goddess. You are deserving of living a luscious life, filled with radiance, abundance and love. Thank you for being willing to embark on this journey with us. Oprah Winfrey once said "The biggest adventure you can ever take is to live the life of your dreams." Your adventure to reclaiming your inner goddess has already commenced. Your journey continues on the very next page...

Safe travels,
Margie xx

Returning To Your Sacred Body
- Sacred Body Awakening

with Stel Coombe-Heath

"You yourself, as much as anybody in the entire universe, deserve your love and affection."
– Buddha

Dear Goddess, yes, I'm talking to you! Because that is who you are, you have merely forgotten your true essence through an enormous distraction called life. Don't get me wrong, this happens to the best of us. We get so caught in the ups and downs of life's delight and tribulations that we forget who we are. We forget we are great beings of light having a human experience; it preoccupies us in the mind and we forget we live in a body.

When we forget we are body, mind and soul, we lose our connection to the divine; we feel shame and guilt for how we look; we try to change who we are; we become preoccupied with how we look in the mirror. We wax our eyebrows, dye our hair, stick on false lashes, starve ourselves to be thin, some go for expensive fillers, liposuction or other extreme measures for acceptance.

The more we compare ourselves with others or the ideal of a perfect body, the more we lose our goddess essence. The only acceptance we need is from ourselves.

Do you ever feel lost, or a sense of not belonging? Are there times where you just cannot feel comfortable in your own body, or do you feel out of flow?

These are all signs of separation between body, mind and soul. Still not sure if you have lost connection with your body?

Here are a few additional signs that you are misaligned with your "soul suit" as I like to call the body.

- You feel a sense of emptiness inside
- You are out of touch with yourself or others
- You consistently feel uncertain of yourself
- Your head is constantly on a merry-go-round from daily stressors
- Your emotions overwhelm you
- You eat mindlessly and sometimes you are unconscious of eating
- You don't feel comfortable in your own skin
- You feel cut off from your body, like it's not a part of you
- You cannot stand looking at yourself in the mirror
- You cannot find one positive thing to say about yourself or body

Separation from the soul suit originates from various factors such as stress, self-judgement, comparison, low self worth, poor body image, just to name a few.

This dissociation of the body causes great distress to the nervous system, which could lead to further feelings of disconnection from yourself and the world around you. When we live purely in our thoughts, the mind takes over and it can take hours for a glimpse of awareness of the body. This imbalance will create a stress response, causing cortisol, our fight-or-flight hormone, to flood our bodies. When we are in stress mode, our minds race as we try to get out of danger, we feel numb and detached from life and the world.

From my work with women struggling with eating disorders, body shame and emotional eating, I see one strong correlation between each client and most women in my community. A clear disconnect with their body, which, much like you, has a unique story behind it. The reason for their disconnect varies from disempowering body beliefs all the way to emotional wounds and trauma. My job is to help them ground into their bodies, heal their relationship with food and reconnect to their true essence of beauty and love.

In order for us to restore balance, we need to ground ourselves and come home to our bodies. This book is about reclaiming your birthright, your goddess status, and in order for you to reclaim your inner goddess, we need to start from the ground up. I'm here to remind you of who you truly are through a process called Sacred Body Awakening.

Before I get into the Sacred Body Awakening process, I would like to take you on a journey of my return to my sacred body.

I struggled to feel at home in my body for decades. In fact, I was at war with my body. From the age of 12, I could not stand the way I looked. I picked my body apart and felt the only way for me to be normal was to be as thin as I could possibly be. I grew up with the belief that being thin was the only way to be accepted. I started abusing exercise, smoking cigarettes and starving myself all to shrink to the smallest size that I could be. The more I tried to change my body, the more insecure I felt around people. I created my own disconnect. This cycle continued for decades. I developed binge eating disorder, body dysmorphia in attempts to make up for my binge eating I abused exercise and developed orthorexia, an unhealthy obsession with eating healthy. Even though I felt trapped in a body I hated, I disassociated myself from her with every opportunity I got.

I hit bottom in 2018. I sat on my pantry floor with tears running uncontrollably. The shame I felt in my body and my obsession with being thin created a complete hatred for my body. I just wanted to be "normal" around food. Through my obsessive behaviour to control my body, I lost my sacred connection to her, I lost my goddess essence. I eventually asked for help. It took a lot of unravelling in old beliefs and behaviour patterns to eventually heal my relationship with food and my body.

Through my healing journey, I delved deep into my spirituality. I practiced yoga and meditation daily and relied on my energy healing training to work on myself. I realised my need to restore the imbalance in my root chakra to ground myself; I needed a sacred body awakening.

My journey might be very different to yours, however the journey back to self and goddess status starts in the physical body. If the connection to the body is lost or damaged, we need to find a way back home, besides we have nowhere else to live, so we might as well make peace with it.

When we feel at home in our own skin, we can heal at all levels and own our power.

The process of coming back to our bodies is called grounding. Grounding or earthing is the practice of energetically connecting back to the earth through your body. Research has found that grounding is an effective strategy against chronic inflammation (1), pain reduction, and improvement in mood. (2)

When we forget we are body, mind and soul, we lose our connection to the divine.

The root chakra keeps us grounded and facilitates the sacred body awakening. The root chakra sits at the bottom of our spine and governs our sense of safety and security. When it's out of balance, we can neglect ourselves and feel like we don't belong, it can affect behaviours in eating patterns, food cravings, aggression, addiction, feelings of depression. When we find balance in the root chakra we feel grounded settled, and ultimately comfortable and satisfied with our bodies.

The base or root chakra is "grounded" in the earth element and handles our basic needs for support and stability, all the things we need to feel at home and stay connected to self and our soul suit.

Let's take a moment to connect to your root chakra. You can follow the instructions below or listen to the guided visualisation meditation in the resources section by going to
https://reclaimyourinnergoddess.com.au/resources

Find a quiet space where you won't be distracted or disturbed.

Sit on the floor or on a meditation pillow.

Find a straight spine, close your eyes, bring your awareness to the weight of your body resting on the floor or pillow, tune into your breath, become aware of the rise and fall of your chest and belly. Feeling the air entering your lungs nourishing your body and activating your 'rest and digest' nervous system.

Take a deep breath into your belly, fill your lungs and sigh out all the air. Continue this cycle to allow you to let go and soften. Take a moment to connect to your body, to come home to your body, so much of life takes us away from this safe and sacred place.

Take a moment to return home to yourself place your hand on the back of your sacrum (the triangular bone at the base of your spine)

Imagine the colour red between your hand and your sacrum. Allow this colour to come alive, spinning like a disk in a clockwise direction.

As the root chakra spins, you feel it opening and expanding downward towards the earth. Imagine red roots growing down your legs into the earth.

Spend a few moments here embracing the emotions that arise from feeling grounded in the root chakra.

When you are ready to come back to the room, deepen into your breath, wiggle your fingers and toes and finally, open your eyes.

Take a moment to journal what you experienced through the root chakra.

Now that you have experienced the root chakra, you will have a greater understanding of why this chakra can be a powerful tool to reconnect with your body.

When the flow of energy is restricted from the root chakra, it becomes blocked. A blocked root chakra switches on the fight, flight or freeze response, forcing our heads to take over, resulting in the disconnection of the mind, body and ultimately soul.

To return to your inner goddess status, we need to rebuild our relationship with our bodies through the root chakra, starting now in my sacred body awakening process.

I hope you are ready to get raw and real. This will be an easy and fun process. There is no way to mess it up, just a whole lot of a-ha moments and the start to radical mind-body awareness.

Let's dive right in so that you can love the skin that you are in!

Take care of your body. You have nowhere else to live.

The Sacred Body Awakening

We will now start a journey home, back to your body so that you can feel more connected, safe and more importantly, find safety and comfort in your body.

I divided the sacred body awakening into four steps, each step getting you closer to true connection with your body. I will guide you every step of the way through different activities. All you need is an open mind and the willingness to face your inner blocks, keeping you from staying grounded and connected.

Step One: Sacred Awareness

Do you have a relationship with your body? Do you ever consider that there should be a relationship with the thing we live life in? Interesting thought? We have relationships with people, work, exercise, food, our phones (yes that's a thing, not romantically, but there is still a relationship).

The definition of a relationship is how two or more things are connected. When we look at our human building blocks, we are body, energy, mind, emotions, and soul. Whether we like it or not, we have a relationship with it.

Any relationship needs nourishment. If you stopped nourishing a romantic relationship or friendship, it sure would not stay a healthy one. In fact, that relationship will probably die out and finally fade out of your daily thoughts.

In order to make changes within ourselves, no matter the size, we need to make space for it. If you had to add any changes to life without making room for it, you will become overwhelmed and will most likely throw in the towel. We need to create a space from our programming around our bodies. Programming is the paradigm we created around how we see our body, the beliefs, thoughts and feelings we have for them.

What is your body paradigm? If you asked me this question 4 years ago, I would have said "I wish I could make it smaller, I hate my body". I felt trapped in a "fat body" that I wanted nothing to with. I avoided the mirror at all costs. On the occasions when I faced the mirror, all I could see was ugly. I would pinch my belly and hips and wished for a do-over, a way to start again in a perfect body.

Everyone has a body paradigm, because we live with our bodies 24 hours a day, we will inevitably have an opinion, feeling or thoughts about them.

The below exercise is aimed at uncovering your body story /paradigm. This helps you step back and create awareness about this relationship. It is not intended to make you feel bad about yourself, only to shine a light on where you are at right now. Awareness is key, and that's why this step has been called sacred awareness.

Side note: when I discovered my body paradigm, I cried ugly tears for what felt like hours, I could not believe how I was speaking to her, how I was treating her, how I hated her.

When I realised that this was my reality 24/7, I knew I needed to make a change. This exercise is what drove me to eating disorder recovery.

If a similar experience comes up for you, just know that I've got you!

In step two of the sacred body awakening, you will discover a powerful way to let go of anything that does not serve you in your paradigm.

Sacred Awareness:

Start my finding a quiet space and practice the grounding root chakra visualisation set out earlier in this chapter. Once you feel grounded, grab a pen and paper let's map out your current body paradigm.

For this exercise, you will turn to your beliefs about your body. Some beliefs you will want to keep, others will not serve you and will want to throw out, as they might not serve you any longer.

1. Before reading this book, did you believe you had a relationship with your body?
2. If you answered yes, how would you describe this relationship?
3. If you answered no, what have been your current thoughts preventing you from seeing this relationship? (side note: don't feel bad if you didn't relate to your body at all. This was me for a very long time and this process will help you find that relationship).
4. How many times a day do you feel like you are in your body?
5. How often do you forget to breathe?
6. Do you look at yourself in the mirror or do you avoid it?
7. What words do you use to describe your body to your friends?
8. What thoughts do you have about your body parts?
9. Do you wish there were parts of your body you could change?
10. What actions do you take to physically change your body? (eg. changing hair colour, botox, skin fillers, exercise and dieting etc.)
11. Do you feel safe?
12. If you already claimed back your crown as goddess, how would you feel about and treat your body?

Bonus task: Keep a thought diary for a week and document automatic thoughts about your body. You will recognise these when you look in the mirror, when you feel overwhelmed, when you feel low in energy. What are the thoughts feeding your body paradigm?

Now that you are aware of your body paradigm, you might be flooded with mixed emotions, tears or deep unexplained feelings about this relationship. There might be an undeniable awareness that might not have been there before, and that's okay. Sacred awareness is key to move forward on your journey to reclaiming your inner goddess.

Sending you so much love and light for completing this exercise, facing the truth can be painful at times and I honour you for doing this work. Showing up for yourself and taking action is how we effectively make change.

Namaste.

"Sometimes the greatest miracle is being able to face exactly where you're at and say: This is where I am, no running, no hiding. There's gold for me here, and I intend to find it, no matter what." Unknown

Step Two: Sacred Release

Wow, if you have made it this far, I know radical shifts in your feelings towards your body are imminent.

If you somehow missed the sacred awareness exercise, I highly recommend going back to complete it. The sacred awareness process will help you move through the rest of the steps in the sacred body awakening process.

A large part of transformation is stepping out of the old and into a brand new version of yourself. We have uncovered all your beliefs, thoughts and feelings towards your soul suit and in the Sacred Release phase, you get to shed unwanted elements from your body paradigm.

This step is by far the most liberating. When we let go of things that do not serve us, we create space to embrace what we really want and how we really want to feel. Letting go will help you feel safe in your own skin and open to embrace a new version of yourself and heal on a soul level.

Are you ready to let go and grow?

Sacred Release:

For this exercise, you will need:

- a pen and paper,
- your answers from the sacred awareness exercise
- a red or white candle,
- a small bowl of water
- a safe fire pit (optional)

Find a comfortable, seated position and put your hands in the bowl of water. This will help ground you back into your body and it serves as a symbolic gesture of washing away that which does not serve you.

Send a few moments feeling the sensations of the water. What is the temperature? What does it feel like on your skin? Does this bring up any memories or emotions?

Close your eyes and allow this breath practice to guide you to a grounded frame of mind ready to release. You can listen to this guided letting go practice in the resource section of https://reclaimyourinnergoddess.com.au/resources

Breath Practice

Take a moment to notice the quality of your breath. Allow the breath to travel down to the base of your spine.

Imagine the colour red in your root chakra. Allow this colour to come alive, spinning like a disk in a clockwise direction.

In your mind's eye, picture yourself feeling safe, protected and grounded.

From this safe space, inhale and say the word "Let".

On your exhale, say the word "Go".

Repeat this mantra 10 times or as long as you need to activate your "letting go" energy.

When you are ready, open your eyes.

Pull out your sacred awareness answers and highlight the elements that are no longer serving you.

On a fresh piece of paper, write down a forgiveness statement for each element. For example, if you have been saying "I hate my body" write down "I forgive myself for hating my body."

This forgiveness is the most powerful practice you can adopt. Do not skip out on this exercise, you will be amazed at the shifts in your energy.

Ho'oponopono is a Hawaiian spiritual practice of forgiveness. The repetition of the word "pono" means "doubly right" or being right with both self and others. It is a process of forgiving others and ourselves in order to heal on an emotional, physical and spiritual level.

We will now use the Ho'oponopono mantra as a forgiveness ritual.

Read out your forgiveness statements and when you are done with your list, repeat after me:

"I'm sorry"
"Please forgive me"
"Thank you"
"I love you"

Light your candle as you continue to say this mantra.

Imagine the flame from the candle absorbing each negative element and any feelings of guilt or shame attached to those elements.

If it is safe to do so, burn your paper and allow any feelings of forgiveness to wash over you.

Bonus task: Repeat the Ho'oponopono mantra for the next week to release any residual energy attached to your forgiveness list.

Release work can be extremely tiring. Allow yourself to process whatever comes up for you in the next few days. You might experience a sense of emotional detox through this process, your body might react by feeling fatigued or hyperactive, or your mind might become overactive or you might experience strange dreams. In extreme cases, you might feel slightly fluey.

Just know that these symptoms are the body's way to release suppressed emotions, make sure to allow for rest, drink plenty of water and spend time in nature to help support you through this release.

If you feel you need to repeat the sacred release process before you move on to the next step, follow your intuition and take the time you need to release as much as you can to make space for your sacred body awakening and journey to your inner goddess.

Step Three: Sacred Agreement

I'm super proud of you for facing your truth and releasing your past body paradigms. The work you have done so far as part of your sacred body awakening was facing a harsh reality of your past and letting it go.

The amazing news is that you now have the power to shift your body paradigm. You now have the power to rewire your thoughts, emotions and behaviours toward your soul suit and that is super powerful.

Oprah Winfrey once said, "The greatest discovery of all time is that a person can change his future by merely changing his attitude."

Are you ready to form a new attitude through the sacred body agreement?

Sacred Agreement

For this exercise, you will need:

- a pen and paper,
- your answers from the sacred awareness exercise

Stand with your feet firmly planted on the earth, we're going to get into an optimal healing state through breathwork. When we are grounded in a relaxed state, loving intelligence emerges.

Close your eyes and feel the effect of gravity on your feet. Allow your root chakra to come alive in a ruby red hue and imagine this read travelling down your legs and into the earth.

Bring one hand in front of your mouth, take a deep breath in and exhale into your hand as if you are steaming up a mirror activating an ancient breath technique called the Ujjayi breath (a powerful breath used to switch on the rest and digest nervous system). Keep your hand in front of your mouth and keep exhaling with the same sound.

When you are comfortable with the sound, close your mouth on an exhale and keep making the sound on the exhale with your mouth closed. Repeat for 10 breath cycles or until you feel grounded and relaxed.

On a new piece of paper, write down the body story you grew up with.

- How has that shown up in your life?
- What is the evidence for this being true?
- Could this belief be an exaggeration of the truth?
- What do you think is the positive VALUE behind that body story?
- Do you share that value?
- Does this belief serve you in ALL situations in your life?

Pull out your sacred awareness answers and highlight the elements that you want to keep. These are the base beliefs and emotions that make you feel good about your body, the foundation of having a great relationship with her.

From you the qualities you want to keep and the positive value in your body story you just uncovered, how can you create a new body story that includes YOUR values?

Create your new Sacred Body Statement:
"I am _____"

Repeat this new body statement to yourself every morning and every time you feel disconnected from your body. Building new beliefs requires repetition of new thoughts and your new body statement.

Make a Sacred Agreement to fully embody your new body story and dispel any old limiting beliefs that will hold you back.

When you catch yourself thinking negatively of yourself or your body, question whether that thought aligns with your new body statement and if it does not allow yourself to think the next best thought to get you closer to your new body paradigm.

Bonus task: Create a screen saver of your Sacred Body Statement and save it on your phone as an extra reminder during the day. Another option is to record your body statement and listen to it a few times a day. Create little reminders all over the house and your workspace that will help you solidify your new body paradigm.

You did it, you just shifted a major belief that has kept you stuck in various patterns of disconnect or dissatisfaction with your soul suit. There is unlimited power in breaking through limiting beliefs and reconnecting with your body.

A belief is formed through a combination of our thoughts and experiences that support those thoughts. Now that you have your new Sacred body statement, it's up to you to think and live this statement every day. You can't change the past, but you can change the interpretation of the past by thinking and acting in a new way. Imagine a loving relationship with your body, feel into the universal love and keep your sacred body statement close to heart.

When I support my clients in my programs to heal their relationship with food and their bodies, I help them easily shift their energy into feeling and living their new beliefs through this exact process. At first, they feel overwhelmed or don't believe that they can feel differently about themselves, but through this work, they start seeing themselves and their body in a different light.

Are you ready to take this one step further, to become empowered in your body and love the skin you're in? I'm excited to show you how in the Sacred empowerment step.

"Remember, you have been criticising yourself for years and it hasn't worked. Try approving of yourself and see what happens." -Louise L Hay

Step Four: Sacred Empowerment

French writer, feminist and philosopher Simone de Beauvoir one said "To lose confidence in one's body is to lose confidence in oneself."

So far you have brought awareness, forgiveness and totally refurbished your old body paradigm. There is now space for a grounded and empowered new you.

The sacred empowerment step is specifically designed to build back your confidence in your body, step into your power and become the goddess you always were. She was just hidden in the shadows of your old paradigm.

I'm excited for you to take this step, form a deeper connection with your body and ultimately with yourself.

Sacred Empowerment

This step is best executed barefoot, so that you can ground back to the earth through your root chakra.

You will need:

- A quiet space outside
- Your sacred body statement

You can listen to this guided sacred empowerment practice in the resource section of
https://reclaimyourinnergoddess.com.au/resources

Sacred Empowerment Practice

If possible, take off your shoes and take a walk in nature. Feel the ground beneath your feet and the earth's loving energy all around you.

Find a quiet spot and stand firmly on the ground. Close your eyes and repeat the following mantra out loud.

"I'm here in my body and all is right in the world"

Allow the words to envelop your cells and gently repeat your sacred body statement five times.

Breathe deeply and exhale completely and become curious. What does your body feel like? What's it like being in your skin? Take this time to revel in and give thanks to your amazing human form, this amazing gift that takes care of you in so many ways without you having to think about it.

In essence, she is a magical being, accompanying you on this earth journey, housing your goddess essence.

Take a moment to place your hands on areas of your body that you dislike or have picked on in the past, feel into these parts with compassion and understanding that these parts are what make you human and they reflect your life experiences.

Take your time to move through every part that you may have disliked in the past and send warm, loving thoughts of thanks to these areas. If there are any areas where you feel tense, breathe lovingly into it and give yourself time to relax further.

Repeat the following affirmations either out loud or in your mind.

- Being grounded and whole makes me beautiful. I can get there just by being still, breathing, listening to my intuition, and doing what I can to be kind to myself and others.
- My body deserves to be treated with love and respect.
- I appreciate my body for all she does for me
- Accepting myself as I am right now is the first step in growing and evolving.
- I trust the wisdom of my body.

- I love and respect myself.
- Thighs, thank you for carrying me to where I want to go.
- Belly, thank you for helping me digest.
- Hips, thanks for supporting my body
- Arms, thank you for allowing me to hold my loved ones.
- Skin, thank you for protecting me.
- Body, if you can love me for who I am, I promise to love you for who you are.

Take a moment to relax and soak up the words from these affirmations. Repeat any or all if you feel called to do so.

When you are ready to come back, deepen into your breath, wiggle your fingers and toes and finally, open your eyes.

Take a moment to journal what you experienced through the empowerment process.

Bonus task: Support your body every morning by asking, "How do you feel and what do you need?"

This has been an incredible honour to guide you through the Sacred Body Awakening. It is my hope that you have found your body, rebuilt the relationship you have with her, through grounding and strengthening your root chakra.

While returning to your sacred body, you got raw and real through the awareness of your now past relationship with your body. You released your old body paradigm through forgiveness, chose a new shared body statement and empowered yourself by forming a deeper connection with self, resulting in radical mind-body awareness.

This journey takes honesty, releasing old beliefs and the willingness to see things differently. You are a true goddess for taking on this brave journey of reclaiming your inner goddess by reconnecting with your body. I'm super proud of how far you have come! As I always say to my clients, this is only the beginning. You now have the power to show up more powerful than you have ever been- and that is magical.

You are now ready to take your next step in reclaiming your inner goddess in the next part of your journey set out for you in Chapter Two through the Sacral Balancing process by Ingrid Galloway.

Thank you so much for sharing your energy with me through the Sacred Body awakening process. Don't ever let life or the things in it dampen your inner light!

Sat Nam (Truth is your name)
Xx
Stel

References:

1. https://www.ncbi.nlm.nih.gov/pmc/articles/PMC4378297/
2. https://pubmed.ncbi.nlm.nih.gov/30448083/

Resources:

To access the resources mentioned in this book go to
https://reclaimyourinnergoddess.com.au/resources

Celebrate Your Love
By Balancing Your Sacral Chakra

with Ingrid Galloway

"A relationship is like a house. When a lightbulb burns out, you do not go and buy a new house; you fix the light bulb."
– Unknown

Have you been feeling snappy of late, frustrated that you haven't been having enough sex? Or perhaps you are unable to ignite that desire for your partner of many years? Life feels so bland, and you want to get your spice and juiciness back!

Amidst the rapid pace and daily demands of life, taking time to indulge in pure pleasure is rarely included on our to-do list, or it is the first to be removed once we get busy. When was the last time you did something just because it made you feel good?

If we never allow pleasure, we can become numb and forget how to feel. We become snappy like the crocodile, lashing out from this unfulfilled space within. If we overindulge, always looking outside of ourselves for something to feed our sensual desires, in time our surface pleasures lose their appeal, or can even become unhealthy addictions. Sensations are most pleasurable when in balance.

One way to increase real pleasure and love in your life is by balancing the Sacral Chakra.

In ancient Indian sciences, chakras are the circular vortexes of energy that are placed in seven different points on the spinal column, and all the seven chakras are connected to the various organs and glands within the body. These chakras are responsible for distributing the life energy, which is also known as Qi or Praana.

Whether you believe chakras exist in a literal sense, or metaphorically, by understanding them, they can be a useful tool for navigating our complex emotions, to remove suffering by bringing them into balance.

The Sacral Chakra is the second Chakra we have. Its Sanskrit name is Svadhisthana and translates to "One's own dwelling". It is represented with the colour orange, and water is its element. The Sacral Chakra governs the adrenal glands; regulates the immune system and metabolism. Specifically, it governs the sexual organs, ovaries / testicles, bladder, bowel and lower intestines.

This Chakra is about feeling and sexuality. When it is open, your feelings flow freely and are expressed without you being overly emotional. It influences your creativity, gut instinct, and confidence in artistic expression. It influences how inspired you feel, the general joy and pleasure in life, satisfaction in a romantic relationship, and your ability to express your emotions. When it's not in balance, it affects your day-to-day life in many ways. Let's have a look at the symptoms and how you can alleviate those.

Some of the Underactive Symptoms of unbalanced Sacral Chakra:

- Feeling unemotional or unexcited
- Feeling lack of desire or passion
- Depriving yourself of pleasure
- Being unable to focus
- Feeling insecure or having low self-esteem
- Experiencing sexual repression
- Feeling jealous often
- Feeling guarded
- Being unable to focus
- Feeling out of touch with creativity
- Feeling detached from your emotions

- Comparing yourself to others
- Feeling out of sorts often
- Feeling shy or timid
- Displaying poor social skills

Some of the Overactive Symptoms of unbalanced Sacral Chakra:

- Feeling overly ambitious
- Experiencing compulsive behaviours
- Feeling overly emotional
- Experiencing emotional dependency
- Having trouble setting boundaries
- Experiencing sexual addiction
- Feeling hypersensitive
- Having an excessive sex drive
- Overindulging
- Acting dramatic often
- Experiencing exercise addiction
- Having frequent mood swings
- Experiencing frequent lower back pain
- Feeling tense or frustrated

When you have manifested a balanced sacral chakra, you will be able to experience life to its fullest, to truly create and enjoy an intimate relationship, and have stimulated imagination and creativity.

My Story

Sitting by the window of a small cafe called Ashfield Apothecary in the inner west of Sydney, drinking their yummy bush chai latte and feeling the weight of the cast iron teapot as I poured the liquid gold, I wondered how to write my story. I know that I have a big story which may move you, which you may relate to, and which you may be able to learn from. However, it will leave me feeling vulnerable and open to being judged by others.

The Girl From Indonesia

I came from a humble home in Jakarta, Indonesia. I was born in 1975 as a single child to a very religious and busy family. Apart from work and school life, it seemed like we spent most of our lives at church.

Growing up, I can remember being continuously pushed by my Mami to study. Some Indonesians call their Mums "Mami", because of the Dutch influence we have. (Indonesia was conquered by the Dutch for 3.5 centuries).

She wanted me to be successful so badly that she put me through various courses and extra-curricular activities that were arduous and stressful. These included learning the English language, piano, organ, singing, and since Junior High School (year 7), mathematics, physics, and chemistry were added to the list I had to do. I had to practice music one hour per day and I dreaded it.

As a result, I only knew how to study and not play. I remember that I didn't even have the desire to do active play and reverted to reading a lot of books (whether it's for study or relaxation). For a long period of time, I felt rather stupid, especially in learning math, physics, and chemistry. I tried asking my teachers to help me during lunch breaks and got tutoring from my clever cousin. Those subjects were simply not my strength.

My life was not balanced. I felt that something was always missing, and I became very rebellious. I was also very disrespectful towards my Mami. I screamed at her daily and yelled out "I hate you!" often.

Some of my Aunties who came to live with us for several years, or visited for a few days, observed how I dreaded the study, and advised my Mami that children need to play. Playing is natural and healthy for their development. As my Mami felt that my Papi was too quiet and didn't enforce child education, she 'had to' step up and be the authoritarian one.

My parents did their best to educate me with their good values, but I tried my best to rebel, as I felt I wasn't being accepted as my true self. I suppose my soul didn't like being suppressed.

I observed that my Papi was such a loving generous man, but also a quiet man who was the master of his own emotional suppression. He expressed his stress when driving. He was an excellent driver, but when fed up, he would suddenly hit the accelerator and speed up the car, leaving my Mami feeling scared for life. I was fine though, as I trusted his driving completely and knew that he needed to blow off some steam.

My Papi passed away quickly (within 24 hours) when he was very young, at 51 years of age from a brain aneurysm, after I had moved to Australia. I had a feeling that the years of suppressing emotions (because of his financial, marital and life stresses) eventually got the best of him. In my reflection time, I observed that his approach to life taught me the importance of expressing myself and the negative impact of emotional suppression.

For several years now, in my self-healing journey, I came to understand that my Mami tried to live her life through me. This is very damaging. She couldn't play piano, nor organ, couldn't sing very well, nor speak English. She wanted all those for herself to be able to serve God better, but believed she was not being gifted with such talents by Him.

She strongly believes that I am talented with all the above (after many years of study/practice), yet I stopped serving God with my talents (especially after my divorce to my first husband), and she considered that a waste, an embarrassment and a disappointment.

There were uncountable times that she projected shame and guilt with her messages throughout the years because I didn't do what she wanted me to do. Perhaps intentionally (as a method of manipulation), or non-intentionally (as a habitual fall-back mechanism).

My understanding, accepting and loving second husband said something BIG about this matter: "Who am I to say that you are not using your talents? You are doing so many things to make people relax, heal and strengthen their relationships, isn't that a talent?"

There's immense amount of shame and guilt projected at me, as I have been compared to my cousins, Mami's friends' children, and other people, frequently from childhood until now, that they are smarter, more successful than me and care about their parents and Mami, (even though they are not her biological children) a hell of a lot more than me. As I don't look after my Mami as per the typical expectation of Indonesian society.

By now, you probably would have guessed that a couple of my big emotional baggage statements are: "I am not good enough" and "I am not worthy of my mother's love."

Sometime ago, I came across a post about Kahlil Gibran, the Lebanese-American poet, painter, and philosopher (January 6, 1883– April 10, 1931), who wrote poignantly about parenting advice, and what may be the finest advice ever offered on the balance of intimacy and independence in a healthy relationship. This piece sings well to my soul:

"Your children are not your children.
They are the sons and daughters of Life's longing for itself.
They come through you but not from you,
And though they are with you,
yet they belong not to you.
You may give them your love but not your thoughts.
For they have their own thoughts.
You may house their bodies but not their souls,
For their souls dwell in the house of tomorrow,
which you cannot visit, not even in your dreams.
You may strive to be like them,
but seek not to make them like you.
For life goes not backward nor tarries with yesterday.
You are the bows from which your children as living arrows are sent forth.
The archer sees the mark upon the path of the infinite,
and He bends you with His might that His arrows may go swift and far.
Let your bending in the archer's hand be for gladness;
For even as he loves the arrow that flies,
so He loves also the bow that is stable."

As painful and traumatic as it was, (I went through years of therapy and soul searching for it, and openly admit that I have "Mum issues"), I am grateful for my conditioning. It taught me the value of hard work, what not to do in parenting and what not to say in a relationship. I learnt to accept that my Mami did the best she could with what she knew. Her reality is different from my reality. We are good people, but simply very different.

The big lesson here is acceptance. Perhaps, if you experienced a similar experience growing up, you can learn acceptance as well.

Another lesson is to set boundaries with people that are close to you. If they do not lift your spirit, are judgmental or cannot accept you for who you are, there is no reason for you to be completely vulnerable and tell them everything about yourself. Even family members. Treat them with respect, as you would with fellow human-beings, but you don't need to give them your heart and soul.

Learning those two major lessons helped to lessen my level of reactivity. I strive to respond to a situation instead of reacting, as there is a big difference between reacting vs responding.

I pray to God that I won't repeat the cycle by projecting my traumatic experience to my children. However, I need to acknowledge that I am only human. That my fallback mechanism easily reverts to what I have learnt for many years, which includes projecting shame and guilt.

Part of my journey is to unlearn my stuff. To unlearn my baggage. Deep inside I have this inner knowing, that even though right now I am opening myself up to criticism from others, by being vulnerable, a lot more people will be able to relate to my story and be inspired to change for their own self-healing. To be encouraged to unlearn the nasty stuff. To be supported by being authentic in their own journey towards balance.

So, what baggage can you unlearn?

Moving To Australia

By the age of 21, I moved to Australia to marry my first husband. We were pen pals for 6.5 years (yes, there were a lot of letters flying around between Australia and Indonesia, and expensive phone calls). We were in love and even though we were young; we decided to get married.

One of the reasons for me to get married so young was to escape from my mother. I love my immediate family, big extended family, and friends- however, home had not felt like home for a long time. My Mami said that I was too Western minded to be an Indonesian, and I guess she was right.

Growing up, as a teenager, unlike many other teenagers, I never asked my parents to buy me a motorbike or a car. I always wanted to go abroad. And in my mind, I always wanted to marry a foreigner. In my culture, typically children will live in their parent's house until they get married.

Back in junior high school, I started pen-palling a couple of people from the back of a magazine. Nobody lasted long, except for Arman (not his real name). He was from Jakarta as well but went to high school in Sydney and he was feeling lonely, hence looking to write letters to someone in Indonesia.

For 6.5 years we wrote to each other, fell in love, and eventually decided to get married, when I was 21. He asked if I would like to move to Australia, or would I like him to move back to Indonesia? Because it was always in my dreams to live overseas, I quickly said that I would make the move, because he already had a steady job. It made little sense for him to start from scratch in Indonesia.

I was very determined to get married, even though my Papi thought I was too young. I had a few boyfriends before I got married, so, it's not like I had no experience in being in a relationship, but there were no red flags entered my radar, when Arman said, "Ingrid, when you move here, you must change your way. It cannot be the Indonesian way of doing things anymore, you need to change." Naively, I answered, "Oh yes, yes, no problem."

He came from a broken family, and my family raised some concerns about that. I quickly defended him though as I am the type of person who doesn't discriminate against background, may it be religion, family origin and so on.

In hindsight, knowing what I know now, I should have taken him to a few therapy sessions, with a psychologist or a coach, to make sure that we worked on our childhood baggage, to dissolve various issues and prepare us mentally for a long and loving marriage.

But no, I was young and naïve, didn't know anyone in Australia (apart from one cousin on my Papi's side) and only did a couple of premarital counselling with our old Minister from church, which was a God-centred approach.

Soon after we got married in Australia, I went back to Indonesia to apply for a permanent residency. Back then in 1996, it was reasonably quick and easy to get it. As long as you have proof of a genuine relationship, filled out some forms and paid a minimal fee, you'd wait for about 6 months in your country of origin, and you'd have no problems.

It was the waiting game that started the killing season of our relationship...

Whilst waiting for my Australian permanent residency approval in Jakarta, I reconnected with some of my high school best friends and we liked to party. With my close friends and their friends, I went clubbing and had the best time of my life! Or so I thought.

Arman was getting more frustrated and angrier with me as I couldn't answer his phone calls as I was spending time with my friends. It started a vicious cycle of me running away from him because he was no longer loving and fun to listen to on the phone, and by me not being able to be controlled by him, he got angrier and angrier.

I was raised in a very religious family and late-night parties and clubbing were not acceptable. It's fair to say that I was rebellious and ravenous for a broader life experience! During my wild nights, I dabbled with methamphetamines (ecstasy). The drugs accelerated my sex drive and inevitably; I began having sex with other men than my then-husband who was overseas.

I wasn't proud of it but looking at it now, it's already a part of my journey. I learn best from experience. And I learnt something that became part of the demise of my marriage. Infidelity. Geez, what a bad, bad girl you were, Ingrid!

After getting my permanent residency, I returned to Australia and reunited with Arman. I didn't come clean right away. But eventually he found out and I had to come clean.

You could only imagine the wrath that came from it. The infidelity triggered massive anger and a controlling and abusive side of him, which I truly believe stemmed from his upbringing. His biological father was an alcoholic all his life, and during his marriage with Arman's mum was unfaithful and abusive, hence the marriage didn't last long. As a single mum, she did whatever she could to provide for the kids, and I admired his love and commitment to his biological mum because of this. They really had it rough. It's massive emotional baggage. Unfortunately, he never got any professional to help relieve the baggage because he didn't believe in therapy.

For almost 10 years, I walked on eggshells, because I let go of my power, due to feeling shame and guilt over what I did. I often justified his anger issues with "I did something very bad to him, so yeah, of course now he's uncontrollably angry", even over menial things like the rubbish bin. Yes, the rubbish bin got dirty, and he blew up. I never realised that a rubbish bin must be so clean that you can eat from it (you get the picture?). Yep, the point was not about the rubbish bin. It's about me following what he wanted.

He would drive me and pick me up to and from places, including work, birthday and farewell parties. If I dared to be 10 minutes late to the agreed time that I must get out of the party, oh there would be fire and explosions. Almost every day that we were married, we were fighting. We truly knew how to push each other's button the wrong way. It's very draining. Every other day he would yell, "I want a divorce! I want a divorce!" (Be careful what you wish for, you may as well get it)

We would break up and he would move out. Then he would apologise, beg me to come back and work things out, and I'd let him back in. The domestic violence cycle continues. The emotional and verbal abuse was practically daily. On three occasions, though, it became physical. I lost my sense of worth completely. After the third time, he moved out. That's it. I have had enough. I'm sure my friends who were supporting me and listened to me crying for years have had enough as well. Even though I believed marriage was a once in a lifetime thing, I simply couldn't take it anymore.

Shame vs Guilt

As you can tell by now, a lot of shame and guilt have surrounded my life. However, I would not like to be stuck as a victim and instead, I would prefer to stand up and bring awareness to others in the topic we don't normally talk about.

Can you differentiate the energy between "I am bad" VS "I did something bad"? The first one is shame based and the latter is guilt based. Shame is one of the most uncomfortable states we have in relationships and in life. Guilt is a feeling of having committed something wrong or failed in an obligation.

Shame is one of the great unspoken words in the world. It's about feeling wrong or not good enough. You feel numb, wanting to hide, disappear and even cease to exist. It is correlated to violence, addiction, aggression, eating disorders, suicide, bullying. Sometimes you may not realise it, but shame is alive and well under your shiny, "everything-is-fine" surface for many of us.

Guilt is different. Can you understand the different meaning in this statement: "I'm not a stupid serial cheater, but by cheating on my partner last month, that was stupid"?

You see, the understanding of the meaning of Guilt vs Shame is very important. "You did a bad thing; you are not a bad person."

The brain processes social pain exactly like it processes physical pain. Shame and humiliation hurt the same as physical pain. For example, if you spill boiling coffee on your hand, the same part of your brain lights up as if I shame you or humiliate you. We are not wired for it. It destroys us.

Intimacy and the potential for shame are close neighbours. To create intimacy, you need to expose yourself to your partner and risk rejection and invalidation. This leaves you open to feeling shame as you seek to be seen, understood, respected, and loved. Fear of shame can keep you from seeking the intimate connection you crave, and even prevent you from surrendering fully to pleasure.

If you think I defend cheaters or people that have done wrong instead of favouring the victims, that's not the message that I'm trying to convey here. In most cases, whether you are the victim or the perpetrator, you are both hurting. You are in pain. Some shame is actually healthy. Because it is important to feel your shame when you've done something wrong, such as hurting others or yourself.

We, aka humans, are about as imperfect a species as you can get. Yet, it's in your imperfections that your perfections lie. You strive for perfection, yet it's the journey that is the golden trip to many lessons in relationships.

Why do people like shaming other people so much?

Because it feeds their ego! The easiest fallback mechanism when we try to protect ourselves is to point and blame others. When we are in pain, shame is a very lethal weapon for discharging our own pain and suffering. It is a tool of oppression. Belittling, humiliating, dehumanising.

The problem is, many of us don't understand that shame doesn't just destroy the victim, it destroys the person who uses it. Do you know that shame is a very dangerous parenting method? You can change a child's behaviour in a second with it! You can have a 'certain look' with a child that could just diminish them.

For children, shame is the threat of being unlovable. For children from newborn through about 4th/5th grade, being unlovable actually means dying. We are most likely to shame when we are scared or in our own shame.

I would like to shine the light on some cultures that highly value shame as a method of parenting. For many who learnt that from childhood, they use it in adult life to control their partner. Can you see how damaging it is?

One of the most common examples of this shaming culture can be found in Asian and Arabic households - when a child turns out to be gay. It is a sad reality that most of them still shame their kids when they show their true selves.

Homosexuality has been a taboo for most countries in the continent, and the repercussions of coming out is being cut off from the family. This leaves the child highly depressed and lacking familial love and support, which can result in substance abuse such as drugs and domestic violence.

This time, I encourage you to do a self-check-in: have you ever been scared about something, then react by shaming others? Have you used shame because of how you were parented? If you had, I don't hold you responsible for information you didn't have. Most people were doing the very best they could. From now on, you can choose a different path.

Reclaim Your Inner Goddess

After reading my story, I invite you to do a self-check-in, in regards to the Underactive and Overactive Symptoms of unbalanced Sacral Chakra. For example, feeling unemotional VS overly emotional; or having sexual repression VS sexual addiction. Then observe the My Story part of the chapter to match my behaviours (and my Mum's, also my ex-husband's) throughout the years. I am sure you will find some underactive and overactive signs.

Now I invite you to look closely at your behaviour throughout your years. Can you relate to anything as above? If you can, congratulations! You are aware. You are now a step closer to your healing. Awareness is the key to healing. As by having an awareness of something, you now have choices on how to heal or balance yourself.

Please note that if you tend to complain about your partner, and have been feeling stuck for some time, you are not alone. When two unique individuals try to connect with each other, challenges are to be expected. It can feel frustrating. The stuck feeling can be the boredom of over-familiarity in the relationship itself. Or it might come from not being able to make your partner give you what you need or desire.

It can also be about something in your own life that's different, such as your creativity, which can get stuck and not flowing as you need it to be. Regardless of what it is, feeling stuck equals feeling powerless.

If you are a creature of habit like most people, when you are stuck, you simply try harder at whatever you were already doing. This may involve avoiding, detaching, nagging, resenting, or annoying. Do you think you will get a different result from doing the same thing over and over again? Absolutely not!

Why don't you try this for a change: take ownership of your "stuckness". It will immediately give you back your sense of self-empowerment and allow yourself to move through it. Instead of trying to change your partner or the situation, try changing your internal state of "stuckness" instead. Creating this change by shifting yourself into a different energetic state is very refreshing for yourself and your partner.

This energy shifting is not to let your partner 'get away with murder', but to help you reconnect with yourself and find your inner goddess. Your inner power. While at the same time gaining a new perspective.

I often say to potential coaching clients that it doesn't matter if their partner doesn't want to come to the coaching relationship. It is possible to create the change with only one party coming to the table.

Yes, it is typically easier for me to help heal the relationship if both parties come and do the work, but it is definitely possible with only one person doing the inner work. As the internal shift in them will also energetically impact on their partner. They will see and feel that my client is being different, which will potentially create a change in them as well.

How To Balance Your Sacral Chakra

Restore balance and proper energy flow to your sacral chakra with following practices:

1. Reconnect with the sacral chakra's element: water. You can take a bath, go swimming, or dangle your feet in the body of water.
2. Be creative. Let your energy flow by exploring new or old hobbies. Try dancing, writing, drawing, or participating in other playful activities.
3. Yoga can help to balance and open your chakras. The best poses for this chakra include the open-angle, frog, pigeon, and goddess poses.
4. Meditation for Sacral Chakra. Sit with your spine and back straight. Relax and breathe deeply. Focus your attention on your sacral chakra and its orange colour for 3-5 minutes.
5. Sacral Chakra Affirmations. Calmly speak positive "I feel" affirmations, such as:
   - "I feel at peace",
   - "I feel passionate",
   - "I feel comfortable with my body."
   - "I am a sexual being I embrace my sexuality",
   - "My sexuality is sacred",
   - "I deserve sexual pleasure",
   - "I have no fear of intimacy" and
   - "I deserve to be loved".

Recite and write the ones you picked daily. This action will help rewire your neural pathway and bring them to reality. When what you think about, say about and action about matched (aligned), the universe will make things happen for you. Here are some more examples of positive affirmations relating to the sacral chakra:

- "I honour my body",
- "I am confident about my body and looks",
- "I honour and express my sexuality",
- "I am confident about my sexuality",

- "I deserved to be treated with respect",
- "I treat others with respect",
- "I respect other people's boundaries",
- "I allow creative energy to freely flow within me",
- "I am independent",
- "I welcome happy and fulfilling relationships into my life",
- "I deserve and experience good things in life",
- "I deserve to enjoy life",
- "I gratefully accept pleasure and abundance" and
- "I am peaceful inside".

6. Aromatherapy. The best essential oils to open and balance this chakra include Orange, Lemon, Lime, Rose, Ylang Ylang, Cardamom, Black Pepper, and Cinnamon.
7. Sacral Chakra Crystal Healing. The Sacral Chakra's complimentary crystals are Carnelian, Ruby, Citrine, Amber, Sunstone, Tangerine Quartz, Orange Calcite, Chrysocolla, Clear Quartz and Fire Opal.
8. Sacral Chakra Foods. Orange foods can help balance your sacral chakra. This includes sweet potato, carrots and orange capsicums.
9. Treatments such as massage and facial. One of my favourite methods to rebalance myself is to receive energy from another therapist. For my clients, I like to place a heavy basalt hot stone below the belly button and on the Sacrum area (you can also accompany it with a Crystal from the above selection). I encourage the act of receiving love without guilt. Simply state to the universe, even without words, that you are grateful to accept pleasure, abundance and you deserve to enjoy life.

Combining these forms of healing for the sacral chakra can be powerful! Here is an example of a morning ceremony that you can do at home, or wherever you are, to start your day right and rebalance your sacral chakra:

1. Soak your feet in a foot spa and warm water, with some sprinkles of Orange, Lime and Ylang Ylang essential oils.
2. Sit with your spine and back straight but relax, breathe in the

aroma from your foot spa deeply, hold a couple of crystals in your hands such as Carnelian and Citrine, and breathe out slowly. Be present, let go of various thoughts and worries, focus your attention on your sacral chakra and its orange colour for 3-5 minutes.

3. Recite some sacral chakra affirmations: "I honour my body. I honour and express my sexuality. I welcome happy and fulfilling relationships into my life. I gratefully accept pleasure and abundance. I feel at peace."

4. Write your affirmations in your journal or dance like nobody's watching whilst singing your new tune of affirmations like nobody's listening. Just have fun with it!

5. Enjoy your breakfast and add an element of orange foods in it. Conclude by saying your gratitude.

Now is the time to ALLOW your senses to genuinely engage with more of the simple and profound pleasures of life. If you feel GUILTY enjoying pleasure for yourself, take a breath and sense where this feeling stems from. Remind yourself - life is meant to be enjoyed, not endured, with yourself and with your partner.

By allowing yourself to engage your senses in things you find pleasurable, you connect with the very essence of life. Every person deserves pleasures in their life. Give yourself full permission (and, in truth, an ultimatum!) to include the experience of pleasure in your world.

Let's reclaim your inner goddess and celebrate your love life by balancing your sacral chakra!

My intention for you at the end of reading this chapter, and by actioning the necessary steps, is to have the balance of intimacy and independence in a healthy relationship. Kahlil Gibran offers advice on the secret to a loving and lasting marriage:

"Let there be spaces in your togetherness,
And let the winds of the heavens dance between you.
Love one another but make not a bond of love:
Let it rather be a moving sea between the shores of your souls.

Fill each other's cup but drink not from one cup.
Give one another of your bread but eat not from the same loaf.
Sing and dance together and be joyous, but let each one of you be
alone,
Even as the strings of a lute are alone though they quiver with the
same music.
Give your hearts, but not into each other's keeping.
For only the hand of Life can contain your hearts.
And stand together, yet not too near together:
For the pillars of the temple stand apart,
And the oak tree and the cypress grow not in each other's shadow."

Resources:

To access the resources mentioned in this book go to
https://reclaimyourinnergoddess.com.au/resources

Secrets to Ageing Backwards

with Eli Huang

"Ageing is not lost youth, but a new stage of opportunity and strength"
– Betty Friedan

My name is Eli Huang and I've been a Beauty Therapist and a Natural Health Practitioner for over 20 years. My passion has always been in ageing and what you can do to look younger and feel healthier. As a beauty therapist, I love to analyse why someone ages quicker than others and what are the secrets of those who look youthful and live long, healthy, happy lives. Over the years, I've studied the science of ageing and how to slow down or even reverse ageing, so our biological age is years or decades younger than our chronological age.

In this chapter, I'd like to share with you the science of why we age and my top 10 tips on how you can slow down the ageing process and start looking younger and feeling healthier.

Why Do We Age?

As humans, many of us have the desire to live to long healthy lives and look younger. So what causes us to age? How can we extend our life by 10, 20 or even 30 years? Most people spend the last few decades of their lives or even more with some sort of dysfunction and disability, suffering from mainly preventable and reversible diseases or on many different pills and medications. We are simply not looking at just our lifespan, the years we are alive or how long we live, but the idea of health span– the years we are disability and disease free and how long we live healthy, vibrant lives.

Scientists around the world are studying what it takes to live a long, healthy life and they have more knowledge than ever before. In many countries around the world, the population is ageing. The average male has a lifespan of 76 years old and for women, around 81 years old. Back in the 1950s, lifespan was in the 60s. According to the World Health Organisation, life expectancy in Japan ranks first. What is Japan doing differently to those in the Western world?

In many countries, chronic illness is at an all-time high, and more than ever, our bodies are full of toxins from the air and environment, foods we eat and the water we drink. Diseases such as Alzheimer's and dementia are rising rapidly. Toxicity and inflammation both play a huge role in the ageing process and are the major causes of our life expectancy.

Research suggests that our life expectancy is not a result of our genes or "inherited", which in fact is the combination of our all our lifestyle habits and mindset (Manen, 2010). These studies show that longevity is associated with various genetic and epigenetic adaptations. We can inherit specific genetic predispositions to a disease or specific gene adaptations that increase our longevity, however we need to understand that even the best genes do not counterbalance your poor lifestyle and diet choices.

The issue with the ageing process is the understanding of whether there is only one or many different factors that cause one to age. Evidence is suggesting that there are only a few reasons as to why we age.

Ageing is the progressive degeneration process of the body, mainly caused by inflammation. Over the years, there has been evidence and studies to show that ageing could be due to chronic inflammation from oxidative stress, mitochondrial damage, endocrine imbalances, deterioration of the immune system, epigenetic changes and age-related diseases.

Inflammation is the leading cause of ageing as well as the cause of every single disease state. Chronic inflammation in the body and especially in the gut or where the solar plexus energy sits is the cause of what goes on inside our bodies that leads to ageing cells, poor physical body functions, chronic diseases and decreased lifespan.

Inflammation is a part of the immune system's response to an outside assault, where it could be virus, bacteria or an injury. We need our bodies to have a strong response to this inflammation to allow us to fight off an attack, however we also need to be able to turn that inflammation off, when the body can't turn off the low levels of inflammation is when we are prone to rapid ageing and chronic illness. This is due to various factors we neglect, such as eating an inflammatory diet, not exercising, not focusing on sleep, not regulating our stress levels. These all lead to inflammation. When you know what is causing the inflammation in the body, you can turn back the biological clock. Human ageing is characterised by chronic, low-grade inflammation, and this phenomenon has been termed now as "inflammageing".

Telomeres

Thanks to science and research, we know that our telomeres start to shrink as we age. Telomeres are stretches of DNA at the end of each chromosome. Telomeres help protect the ends of your chromosomes from damage or fusing with nearby chromosomes. In the process, the telomeres shorten, which is associated with ageing and disease.

They have found that older people with longer telomeres do not experience vascular ageing quite as quickly as those people with shorter telomeres. This means their veins are in better shape and they are less likely to be at risk for conditions like heart disease and stroke.

However, research suggests we can slow down this process or even lengthen our telomeres through better diet and nutrition, stress management and exercise- all of which we will cover in this chapter. It is no longer thought that just because one has bad genes passed down to them by their parents that they will have the same chronic illnesses as in their family. Findings suggest it is all about our diet and lifestyle that affects how these genes are expressed. Research (Balan, 2018) indicates that longer telomeres are associated with health span including fewer illnesses and a longer lifespan.

Solar Plexus Chakra

The solar plexus chakra, or "Manipura" in Sanskrit, translates to "city of jewels" or "shining gem". This chakra has to do with your personality, identity, ego, personal freedom, power and authenticity. It also influences motivation, purpose, willpower, self-esteem and self-confidence so you can move forward on your path in life with courage and inner strength. This is the area of your personal power centre.

The solar plexus governs our digestive system, including the spleen, stomach, pancreas, kidneys, liver and adrenal glands. It also regulates our blood pressure, respiration and our stored emotions. The solar plexus is located in the centre of your abdomen. It sits just below the diaphragm, right behind your stomach, and in front of your aorta, which is the largest artery in your body.

When this chakra is out of balance, it manifests as physical issues of the digestive system, metabolic issues, diabetes, gastric issues, respiratory issues, pancreatitis and anxiety. Emotionally, we become irresponsible, have a need for control, feel helpless, insecure and lose our sense of purpose and authenticity.

When this chakra is balanced and flowing freely with unblocked energies, we are empowered to live with a strong sense of purpose, confidence, and motivation. We can be our truest authentic selves, and we can trust our intuition without any doubt. Once your energies flow more naturally, you can break free from pain, frustration and anxiety.

Strengthen This Inner Digestive Fire

The fire within your third chakra is called 'agni'. We need to keep this digestive fire healthy and alive to help you achieve your goals, desires and intentions in life. By strengthening this third chakra and the powerful fire within your solar plexus, you'll feel more driven towards your goals, where you can change your thoughts into actions. You can achieve anything you set out to accomplish. If you feel stuck or don't know which way to turn to, look within at your gut instincts for some guidance. You can also meditate on this chakra by chanting 'RAM' which will help increase your ability to be able to stand up for yourself, help control negative impulses and allow for greater self-control and power within this chakra.

When your solar plexus chakra is blocked, you may:

- Have low self-esteem
- Feel powerless and weak
- Feel victimised
- Feel unmotivated and directionless
- Find it difficult to take actions
- Feel self-doubt
- Feel helpless
- Feel a lack of purpose
- Have digestive issues
- Suffer from anxiety

When your solar plexus chakra is open, you may:

- Be motivated
- Feel powerful and influential
- Trust your intuition
- Be assertive
- Feel confident
- Reach your goals more easily
- Easily make conscious choices

Once you realise that the solar plexus chakra is all about your personal power and confidence, you are able to discover who you truly are in your true authentic self, let that shine and show it to the world. When you have balanced this chakra, you are able to overcome your fears, master your inner thoughts and make more informed and conscious decisions so you can go out there to follow your own path and create the life you want.

My Top Tips to Ageing Backwards

1. Reduce Stress

Physical, mental and emotional stress are the main causes of illness as it has huge effects on our immune system as it drives up inflammation, the key to ageing and disease. All illnesses come from chronic long-term stress in the body. Our bodies are not meant to handle chronic stress. Most of us are in a constant stressed state "flight or fight response". When our bodies are in this stressed state (sympathetic nervous system) our immune system shuts down. Our bodies are basically in stress from the moment we are born to the moment we die. Therefore, we need to change our mindset and behaviours around this stress and develop techniques and routines to better handle it.

When we're stressed, our bodies start producing the stress hormone cortisol. Cortisol is linked to lower levels of telomerase, and telomerase prevents telomere shortening. Chronic stress also affects our epigenetics, which is how our genes are expressed. There our lifestyle and environmental factors can increase or help decrease stress sin our bodies.

For many people, when they become stressed, they turn to poor diets high in carbs and sugar, cigarettes, alcohol or drugs as a means to handle the stress. However, this makes the body more inflamed and stress and it becomes a vicious cycle. Find out what the stressor in your life is and try to change your attitude or approach to that stress. It is not the stressors that kill you; it is your response to that stressor that impacts your health.

Therefore, a good overall anti-ageing strategy is to reduce stress. It is so important to balance out our neurochemistry by reducing inflammatory foods, changing our mindset and doing physical exercises like yoga, tai chi, dancing and hiking, as well as meditation or breathing.

A study done in 2016 at UCLA (Luders, 2016), where 50 long-term meditators and 50 control subjects were analysed, and the meditators were on average 7.5 years younger than those who didn't meditate. People who do both yoga and meditation have been shown to have significantly reduced rates of cellular ageing as well as longer telomeres and increased longevity.

There are so many studies to confirm that stress is one of the biggest ageing accelerants. When we can manage our stress, we are healthier and live longer.

2. Reduce Sugar Intake

Sugar is the single biggest cause of inflammation in the body. It is the biggest cause of ageing at the cellular level. The World Health Organisation recommends only 6-8 teaspoons (26g) of sugar a day. The average adult consumes around 27 teaspoons a day and that is almost 5 times the recommended daily intake recommended by WHO. Restricting your sugar intake is the key to living a long, healthy life.

Studies show that large amounts of sugar leads to oxidative stress through free radicals in the body, causing inflammation which leads to long-term chronic diseases including diabetes, heart disease, depression and anxiety and Alzheimer (Jacques, 2019). It is the primary cause of stress in our body.

Sugar breaks down the body's collagen, which leads to accelerated ageing and inflammation. When we consume excessive amounts of sugar, the excess glucose in our blood causes the glucose to breakdown the collagen fibres and create more wrinkles and saggy skin.

Sugar is highly addictive, similar to heroin and 8 times more addictive than cocaine! It is one of the most addictive and deadly narcotics out there, yet it is readily available and legal. This is because it causes large amounts of dopamine to be released in the brain. That is why people become highly addicted to sugar. In obese people, they need to consume even more sugar to get the same effect. Sugar is the MOST dangerous drug of the modern times which is still easily accessible everywhere!

Sugar also causes the blood glucose to rise, and research shows that there is a very good correlation between high blood sugar levels and a shorter lifes-pan. And not just type 2 diabetes, but all aspects of ageing.

Avoid processed sugars and the hidden sugars in sauces, bread, salad dressings, canned tuna, canned vegetables, biscuits, yoghurt, sugary drinks. There are also over 60 different names for sugar! Read the labels carefully and avoid common names for sugar such as agave nectar, cane juice, cane sugar, dextrin, dextrose, fructose, fruit juice, glucose, HFCS (High-Fructose Corn Syrup), malt syrup, maltodextrin, maltose, palm sugar, saccharose, sucrose, syrup.

3. Importance of Sleep

Sleep is vital to our health and immune system as well as essential for helping us to look younger and feeling healthier. Sleep is time when your body and mind are repairing itself. When we have a good night's sleep, we feel energised, rejuvenated and refreshed in the morning. Even one night of poor sleep can cause swollen eyes, dark circles, pale skin, increased wrinkles and lines.

When we sleep, it allows our brains to work more efficiently and it's allowing us to encode memories of our daily experiences. Sleep is extremely important as it activates the part of our system in the brain called the glymphatic system, which basically is the brain getting rid of the toxins during the REM cycles or deep sleep cycles which help to optimise our health span. If you don't sleep, you'll basically die after a fairly short period of time. When we sleep, our body regulates itself- our immune systems, bodily inflammation and our appetites are regulated.

How much sleep we get significantly affects and influences our mood, memory, productivity and energy levels. When we sleep, our brains work 10 times harder to remove toxic proteins and debris and are more active when we sleep than during wake times. Lack of good quality sleep over time increases anxiety and our risk for serious chronic health issues such as high blood pressure, diabetes, cardiovascular disease, Alzheimer's weight gain and obesity. Insufficient sleep creates more stress on the body, increases inflammation and weakens our immune system.

Aim for at least 7 to 8 hours of good restorative sleep and avoid screen time at least 30-60 minutes before bed, and especially during the night. A good routine before bed can also help with melatonin production before sleep. When you wake, get some natural sunlight to get your body clock regulated for your sleep-wake cycles.

4. Exercise and Movement

We all know that exercising is great for our health, however, new research shows that exercising is also great for slowing down the ageing process (Carapeto, 2021). However, not all types of exercises are created equal.

You should add endurance and high-intensity interval training to your exercise. Mayo Clinic research showed the best type of exercise is high-intensity interval training, or HIIT. That means you do very short and intense bouts of exercise that raise your heart and respiration rates dramatically. It's the best for promoting longevity, including in older exercisers. These types of exercises can help keep your heart rate up and turn on your longevity genes, helping the cells stay younger and slowing down the shortening of your telomeres. By including aerobic and high interval training, you experience increased telomerase activity, which helps the chromosomes to become longer with at least 20 minutes of exercise daily. For those who poor joints, you can try low intensity such as swimming or walking.

You should also include strength training, weight training and stretching or flexibility, because when we get older our body's muscle mass decreases and this leads to an increase in falls, fractures, osteoporosis and injuries.

Many of us do not exercise or move enough. In a study published in the Lancet (Ekelund, 2016) he shows that sitting for long periods of time or having low physical activity leads to a 59% more risk of mortality, which is similar to that of smoking. When we sit for 3 hours straight, it is like our bodies have smoked half a pack of cigarettes due to the toxic build up in our bodies. By sitting, we shorten our life by 6 years when we sit all day. We need to get moving every hour, for at least 7 minutes and try to walk at least 10,000 steps a day to keep the body fit, mobile and pain free.

Another great benefit of exercising, especially aerobics or even something you love and enjoy, is that it is great for the brain as it helps our brain-derived neurotrophic factor (BDNF) -a chemical that is involved in accelerating the growth of new brain cells.

5. Diet and Nutrition
Our health and how we age are all hugely contributed to by the foods

we eat. Food is not just the calories or energy we need, it's 'information' that can talk to your genes. Food has so many functions, from how it controls your hormones, your immune system and gut microbiome, your brain chemistry, to how it aids your detoxification system.

The ancient cultures got it right when they knew that food really is medicine. When we have a diet rich in whole foods, plant-based foods, nutrient-dense foods, we are basically eating medicine every day for our body. Food is the fastest acting and most powerful medicine you can take to change your life and your health. Within minutes, healthy foods help regulate every single function of your body.

If we eat foods that are highly processed, high in sugar and processed carbohydrates, we cannot expect optimal health. Therefore, the foods we eat either help to create better health or create disease within our bodies. Much of the research now shows that a poor diet is the contributor towards many preventable chronic illnesses such as Type 2 diabetes, many cancers, heart disease, metabolic disease, dementia and much more. When we eat whole foods that are rich is phytochemicals and antioxidants, fibre, good fats and protein, we can prevent, treat and even reverse many of these chronic illnesses. Many foods even fight disease and create better health. So how can we eat a diet that allows us to have a health span that equals our lifespan?

For many, it may require an entirely new diet regime. Introducing some superfoods but still eating junk food will not be the same. Most people in the Western world have a SAD or standard American diet. We need to eat a diet that is rich in plant foods, which contains lots of colourful fruits and vegetables which are high in phytochemicals. You also need to incorporate some good fats such as coconut oil, olive oil, avocados, nuts and seeds and other omega-3 fats such as salmon, sardines, mackerel, anchovies.

For all of us, we want to eliminate the simple sugars and the refined carbohydrates. You want to consume more whole grains that are rich in fibre, like quinoa, brown rice and, and even some full whole-grain breads within your meals and feel really good and satisfied with that. Carbohydrates should come from vegetable sources such as sweet potato and pumpkin, and include healthy fats and protein at every meal. Another tip to better health is to reduce white processed flour and sugar, including any form of artificial sweeteners. The odd occasion or as a treat is fine, instead of daily. Check to ensure we are not eating things in our foods that are pesticides, hormones, antibiotics, additives, preservatives, artificial sweeteners, chemicals, colourings or MSG.

Proteins are an essential macronutrient for our health. Ensure you are getting enough but not too much or not too little. The right amount, approximately for a 70kg person would be around 70grams of protein a day, which should include animal and vegetable protein, and this can be divided throughout all the meals. This can also help us maintain our blood sugar levels, mood and focus.

When it comes to animal protein, it needs to be grass fed as opposed to grain fed. Grass fed regeneratively raised animals are better for our health. Ensure other protein is organic and not pumped full of hormones. If you can eat organic, grass fed and hormone free and wild caught foods, they will create better healthy genes, increasing your health span and addressing most chronic disease issues.

What you eat needs to promote longevity. Use lots of spices, good quality fats, and colourful vegetables in your meals. Vegetables are the phytochemical rich compounds to help reverse ageing. Foods that are great for our gut microbiome, which helps the energy of the solar plexus be more balanced, would be fermented foods such as sauerkraut, kimchi, kefir, and kombucha. Turmeric is great for our immune system as it is rich in curcumin that has a lot of anti-inflammatory and antioxidant properties.

Eat a diet that's very colourful. Basically, eat the rainbow and include foods that are red, blue, purple, yellow, orange, and green. Have lots of healthy fats. When we eat this way, we significantly reduce inflammation, detox our bodies, balances out our hormones, improve your brain chemistry, improve your energy in the cells, provide antioxidant protection to the body to prevent disease and keep you younger for longer.

When you have a consistent healthy diet every day, you will see the long-term benefits of having better metabolism, lowered body fat, better muscle mass, reduced inflammation, better mitochondria (powerhouse energy cells) and improved brain clarity. These are all the things you need as you age, so start eating better and start as soon as possible because food is the most powerful thing on the planet for better health.

6. Reduce Toxins

We live in a very toxic environment, and they can significantly affect our health. Our environmental toxins can damage our DNA and affect our mitochondrial health and longevity.

People living in places with cleaner air quality live longer and healthier. Those who live near chemical factories, big phone and cell towers, polluted industries show risks for chronic illness and premature deaths (Gilderbloom, 2016).

To have a long healthspan and lifespan, we need to avoid environmental toxins as much as possible. This list would be the top 10 environmental toxins which are the most common in our air, water and food to avoid:

1. Pesticides - detected in 50-95% of foods, fruits, vegetables (Pesticides in Food, 2021)
2. PCBs (polychlorinated biphenyls) – found in farm-raised salmon
3. Mould and Fungal Toxins– contaminated houses and buildings
4. Phthalates– in fragrances, plastic wraps, plastic bottles, plastic food containers
5. Parabens–synthetic preservatives found in body care products and cosmetics
6. VOCs (Volatile Organic Compounds) - present in many household products such as water, carpet, paints, deodorants, cleaning products, cosmetics, dry cleaned clothes, air fresheners
7. Dioxins– chemical compounds from waste found in animal fats
8. Asbestos - insulating material used from 1950-1970s. Found in

insulation of floors, ceilings, water pipes, and heating ducts

9. Heavy Metals– such as arsenic, mercury, lead, aluminum, cadmium, which are very common in our environment such as drinking water, fish, vaccines, wood, paint, deodorants, dental amalgams, building materials and soil and fertilisers

10. Chloroform- formed when chlorine is added to water, found in the air, drinking water and some foods

11. Formaldehyde– found in various home products, insulation, tobacco smoke, grocery bags, cosmetics

12. Bisphenol A (BPAs)– found in plastic bottles and plastic containers, package wraps

It is fairly impossible to avoid all environmental toxins today, however you can eat clean and organic foods, avoid processed foods, avoid toxic personal care products which affect our hormonal and endocrine systems, use natural cleaning products around the house, remove any heavy metals in your teeth fillings and filter your water and air. Do what you can to support your body's own natural detoxification system in our toxic world.

7. Brain Health

So we now know that food is a huge influence on our health and genetic expression, but the foods we choose to eat also can change the wiring of our brains, our thoughts, our emotions and behaviours. We want to avoid Alzheimer's and dementia and have good mental clarity until the day we die. Therefore, looking after the health of our brains is vital for health and longevity. This can be by increasing essential fatty acids into our diets.

Omega 3s or essential fatty acids are one of the most important nutrients for the body. They reduce inflammation and are great for brain health. EPA (eicosapentanoic acid) and DHA (docosahexaenoic acid) are good fats found in oily fish and seafood. Omega 3s have been linked to healthy ageing throughout life (Troesch, 2020), and the EPA and DHA have been shown to benefit the body in many areas such as healthy foetal development, the heart and the cardiovascular function, preventing Alzheimer's disease and to help normalise and regulate cholesterol triglyceride levels.

Our bodies do not produce these fatty acids, so our only source is from fish or algae. However, these days a lot of fish are farmed with high mercury and minimal EPA present, therefore, taking a good quality fish oil is essential. Algae oil is a suitable alternative if you are vegetarian or vegan. EPA works to reduce inflammation in our joints, gut and brain and even reducing depression. Taking the right amounts of EPA will allow your joints to move better and even reduce the need for anti-inflammatory drugs (NSAIDs) by 30% in 3 months, help reduce brain fog and improve memory. Our brain is made up of 75% fat and DHA is one of the most prevalent fatty acids in the brain. This explains why our brains do better when we have adequate supplies. EPA would be my number one supplement choice for healthspan and longevity. If you look at those people living over 100, who mainly live near coastal waters, their diets mainly consist of fresh fish and seafood.

Another thing to pay attention to while on the topic of fats are high pro-inflammatory oils such as omega-6 oils such as vegetable oils, corn oils, safflower, soy oils that are highly processed should definitely be avoided. We now know from research (DiNicolantonio, 2017) that inflammation is being caused by the bad fats we consume, therefore we need to reduce inflammation through healthy fats such as omega 3 fats are great for our health and reducing bad or inflammatory fats and oils.

8. Have A Purpose

While I was studying the centenarian patterns around the world, there were some common patterns. Many of them are connected to a higher power, belong to a community group or church group. By having a spiritual connection to a higher power, you are able to feel more connected and present. These people also have a wonderful family connection. They say you need to have at least 3-5 important people in your life. It keeps you real and makes you feel connected and loved by those around you.

Feeling that you have a sense of purpose in life helps you to live longer, no matter how old you are, according to the many reports and studies (Hill, 2014) and observing the centenarians around the world. Finding a purpose in life lowers your risk of mortality above and beyond some other factors which predicts your lifespan. One major study of nearly

7000 participants showed those people with greater purpose in life consistently had lower mortality risks in their lifespan and stayed younger for longer.

There are definite benefits in finding your purpose in life, whether that is to give back to the community, volunteer with charity or looking after grandkids. Having a sense of purpose helps us stay healthier and younger, to keep living and thriving. These centenarians all have a purpose. It is also shown that those who never retire from work also have a purpose and live longer.

Therefore, in summary, we know that our health in reality is not from our inherited genes as we used to think, apart from only a very small minority of genetically determined diseases, the majority of our genes are not what determines our health destiny. We can definitely change the expression of these genes and live long and healthy lives.

By consciously changing our diet so we eat the best food we can, manage our stress better and get good restorative sleep each night and look after our brain health, we can live a longer healthy life. Our day-to-day lifestyle choices are profoundly influential in determining our genetic expression. We know that food is a huge influence on our genetic expression, and the foods we choose to eat affect the wir-ing of our brains, our thoughts and our emotions.

I hope this chapter has provided you with some insights into ageing and how we can take these secrets and tips and reverse the ageing process- even age backwards, so we can become beautiful goddesses that we all deserve to be and live happy, healthy, fulfilled lives that are vibrant, empowered and purposeful.

I have included a 'Health and Abundance Journal' which you can download at (www.reclaimyourinnergoddess.com.au/resources) to reflect on any of the ideas and tips we mentioned in this chapter and of how we can be mindful in making these changes in our health so we can achieve optimal wellness.

References:

Alimujiang, A. e. (2019). Associations Between Life Purpose and Mortality Among US Adults Older Than 50 years.

Balan, E. D. (2018). Physical Activity and Nutrition: Two Promising Strategies for Telomere Maintenance.

Carapeto, P. A.-M. (2021). Effects of exercise on cellular and tissue aging.

DiNicolantonio, J. (2017). Good Fats versus Bad Fats: A Comparison of Fatty Acids in the Promotion of Insulin Resistance, Inflammation, and Obesity. Journal of Missouri State Medical Association, 303-307.

Ekelund, e. a. (2016). Is Sitting Actually the New Smoking?

Gilderbloom, J. a. (2016). How Environmental Toxins Reduce Life Expectancy In Many American Neighbourhoods.

Hill, P. a. (2014). Purpose in Life as Predictor of Mortality Across Adulthood. Psychological Science , 1482-1486.

Jacques, A. e. (2019). The impact of sugar consumption on stress driven, emotional and addictive behaviors. Neuroscience and Behavioural Reviews, 178-199.

Luders, E. C. (2016). Estimating brain age using high resolution pattern recognition: Younger brains in long term meditation practitioners.

Manen, I. V. (2010). "Factors associated with reaching 90 years of age: A study of men born in 1913 in Gothenburg, Sweden". Journal of Internal Medicine 270, no 4 .

Pesticides in Food. (2021). Retrieved from EPA US Environmental Protection Agency: epa.gov

Troesch, B. e. (2020). Expert Opinion on Benefits of Long-Chain Omega-3 Fatty Acids (DHA and EPA) in Aging and Clinical Nutrition.

Resources:

To access the resources mentioned in this book go to

https://reclaimyourinnergoddess.com.au/resources

Reconnect With Your Heart to Live Aligned, Alive and Authentically You!

with Beth Dovey

"Don't ask yourself what the world needs; ask yourself what makes you come alive. And then go do that. Because what the world needs is people who have come alive."
— Harold Whitman

Have you ever found yourself just following the societal norm?

Doing what is expected by you from your family, friends or even government?

Or have you just followed traditions that you have no idea of the purpose for it?

So often I have seen people just living and doing what they have always done without conscious awareness of what they are actually doing, or what they, themselves would actually want.

Often this can be caused from the heart chakra being guarded or blocked and life misaligned with what is important and meaningful to you. This was me for 31 years!

I conformed to what was suggested I should do, the good little Catholic girl, who hardly rebelled throughout school, went to uni, got a job straight out of uni, got married at 21, kids by 23, and 2 more over the next 8 years, while continuing work as a medical scientist and running 2 café takeaway businesses with my ex-husband. (Sounds exhausting? I know!) Then at 31, I finally left my abusive marriage, because I wanted my kids to see what real happiness looked like. Until then, I never stopped to think, "What do I really want?" "What do I love to do?" "What brings me joy and excitement in my life?"

Have you asked yourself these questions, and then unapologetically lived your life by your answers?

Throughout this chapter, I would like to take you on a journey to create awareness of the walls or blocks around your heart chakra. To implement steps every day to help open and keep open your heart to bring abundance and love into your life every single day. I will bring to your awareness, and identify what needs to be healed, so you can continue on your journey to reconnect with your heart and guide you back to your true path where you can live aligned with your values, feel alive and full of zest, and be unapologetically, authentically you!

Over the course of our lives, the human tendency is to stop receiving love. We are ok to give it to people, but stop allowing ourselves to receive. This may be for so many reasons- it may be due to our parents not knowing how to express love and affection to us when we are young, or maybe trauma, maybe religious beliefs that talk about only being in service to others, but not accepting service or love, because that may be selfish, or we don't believe we deserve it. Does that sound crazy to anyone else?

Why wouldn't a beautiful innocent baby that grows and experiences life, not deserve love?

We all start life, our soul, as this divine being, that everyone would agree just deserves love. Yes?

To keep this pathway open to receive love, we humans need to be bathed in love, to grow and thrive and make this world a better place. When love is withheld or blocked, we start stepping away from our authentic self that is living from the heart. This concept of giving and receiving love is pivotal to reopening your heart, and living your authentic path.

Choice

Have you ever heard the statement; "you can't have what you can't language"?

Did you know you have a choice of what you want in life?

Stepping into your power requires you to expand your awareness of the world around you and be curious about what you don't know.

When I left my marriage, one of the keys to my healing and realignment was wanting to experience the world around me. To do this, it required me to choose what I wanted to do. For so long I just went along with what my ex-husband, dad or others wanted. I never felt like I had a choice. The reality we need to understand, is that not choosing, is also a choice. Everything we do is a choice, from what topping you want on pizza, to what car you buy and who you spend time with, to staying in bed all day. I now wanted to choose the experiences. I made good and bad choices, and they were all ok and progress, because, it was still my Choice!

Every chance I had, I would take adventures and explore where I could. I was completely rebuilding my life. I went from having a home and a materialistic, financial and focus of what I'd built over 15 years, to having all my belongings in a few boxes, and with limited finances. On my kid-free weekends, I would jump in my car and travel about a 2 hour radius from where I live. I would walk, run, explore, swim, go to beaches and mountains, do cheeky things my parents and possibly ex-husband would have frowned upon. My journey was to reconnect with what I actually loved and enjoyed. One of my favourite things to do was head down to Byron Bay. I would take my food, a blanket and pillow to sleep in the car. I found a delicious cocktail bar where I would write and journal, enjoy a few different cocktails, people watch and then when I was ready, head back to my car looking over the beach. The first time I did this, I was craving the adventure. It was winter, but I did it anyway. I was woken that morning by piercing light through the car window. I woke to the most magnificent sunrise I have ever seen. It was breathtaking, I had to get out of the car, and just sit and watch in silence and awe, as many others were as well. If anyone spoke it would have ruined it. Even taking a photo of it felt disruptive, and so clearly not present in the moment. At the time I was shamed by a person who I was taking advice from, because he thought I wasn't looking after myself by sleeping in the car. However, I have absolutely no regrets. If I booked a room, I would have never seen that sunrise. The beauty of what I saw will stay with me always. That moment of breathlessness, and intense magnificence is a feeling that is anchored in me and I recall often. We may forget the details of what happened, but we never forget how we felt while doing something we loved or experiencing something new and amazing. Chase more moments like that in your life!

Explore with curiosity and wonder of the world around you. When we have high values of curiosity and wonder, fear will no longer hold as much weight, and therefore will no longer hold you back. The fear of getting it wrong. Fear of being humiliated, fear of asking questions or maybe even a fear of not being good enough. Do any of these fears resonate with you?

When you embrace curiosity and wonder, you move from fear of your survival being threatened, to the energetic vibration of love and joy. 95% of our life force is held in the lower three chakras. When we can open the heart chakra, and receive the joy and love you unlock and open the energetic pathway to connect with the Divine through the higher chakras.

What if you asked more questions in life? When you think someone is angry at you, what if you asked, "are you angry with me?", "Have I done something wrong? ", then you have the answer and no longer need to fear it. Ask more questions and live with curiosity. One piece of advice I was given that was really crucial for my naivety was, if someone doesn't like you asking questions, or they carry on like a fool and not answer your question, they are most likely not speaking from a factual reality. They are just talking with emotions and what serves their ego at the time; so brush it off and don't believe all that they say.

Do you recall hearing adults saying to kids that they should be seen but not heard. Or- Stop asking questions! You ask too many questions!

Asking questions and making mistakes are the way a child learns. It's the way a child continues to grow and become the unique person they are. I believe that if a child thinks of a question to ask, they deserve and need an age-appropriate answer. If a child or person for that matter, has a question in their mind, that they are not given the answer for, from an appropriate source, they will answer that question with their own perspective, and this may not be accurate.

Remember perspective and interpretation of information is individual to every person. We see and take in information that is relevant, a priority or looks or feels similar to our own past experience.

This is how our mind works. Our senses from our body are taking in millions of pieces of information at any one time, however, our mind could not possibly process and interpret all of them. Our mind can only take in 7-9 chunks of information at any one time, so it needs to have a filtering system of what goes in and gets processed and interpreted. This filtering system ensures that we are able to continue to survive and preferably thrive. If there is too much sensory information present in our experience, our brain cannot process it. So the information gets distorted, deleted or generalised in our conscious mind. So… we actually miss a lot of information because it's irrelevant to us.

"We don't see the world as it is…. We see the world as WE are." (Rumi)

Our mind is made up of the conscious and subconscious mind. Only 10% of our mind is composed of the conscious thoughts we know about; and 90% subconscious, thought processes that we aren't aware of. So…90% of the thoughts that are driving your behaviour are actually unknown, or subconscious. How about that!

What meaning are you making?

As humans, we are meaning making machines for everything we do, because we usually don't know what is in our subconscious. We attach a meaning to everything we experience. For example, a girl has a boyfriend who doesn't ring when he said he would, she could put a meaning to that experience as; "he must be busy at work, he does love working." Or maybe she could make it mean that she is not good enough for him and he doesn't make her a priority. Another example could be a child is refused help by their teacher at school and told that they should be able to do the work by themselves. The child then creates the belief that they shouldn't ask for help, and it means they must be stupid.

These types of beliefs that we don't know exist, are limiting us every single day. This is what I help the amazing people I work with to bring to conscious awareness, and change, to get the results they want in their life.

Exercise
Take a few minutes at the end of each day to journal and reflect on the day. Have you achieved what you wanted to achieve today? Do you feel good about yourself? If not why? What's holding you back, what is stopping you from being the best version of you for that day? This will bring awareness to patterns of behaviour.

How we perceive the world is determined by the filters that form the filtering system of our perception are made up of 6 elements. The first is what is a priority to you. Have you ever noticed that when you are looking at buying a red Toyota Corolla, all of a sudden you see red Toyota Corollas everywhere?

Then there is your value system. Your value system is what is actually important to you and you hold high value of the emotional states gained from an experience. For example, a workaholic who's love languages, (Gary Chapman's work) are physical touch and words of affirmations; they will hold lesser value and importance on the need to spend time with their partner every day, because they have such a strong value for work, and the significance and self-worth they get from achieving at work. This could potentially contribute to closing the heart off. Other filters of the mind are belief systems, morals, emotions and past experiences.

How do belief systems and morals effect the way you interpret a situation?

If for example you are a devout Catholic, and have been raised being told that sex before marriage is wrong, this is going to have a strong influence over how you interpret the behaviour of the "cool group" in high school that sleep around and smoke drugs. How we view and judge others and ourself are influenced by all these filters.

Our past experiences really filter our perspective. Let me tell you an analogy I think explains this so clearly.

Three female friends were walking through a market one day. The girl on the right grew up in a family with parents still together, where the father was emotionally present and the males were respectful, protective, supportive and nurturing. The girl on the left grew up in a single mum household, because her dad was violent to her mum for the first 2 years of her life. The mum fled that relationship with her daughter, however the mum was never able to heal the emotional wounds of that experience, and consequently lived the rest of her life as a man hater. The girl in the middle, let's call her Rebecca, was wearing a really funky skirt and enjoying the markets with her friends. A guy walks towards them, holding hands with a girl who appears to be his girlfriend. He remarks "hey, cool skirt!" to Rebecca as he walks past. The girl on the right reacted with, "Oh, how lovely for the guy to make the effort to compliment you when he had his girlfriend there. "

And the girl on the left responded with, "OMG, what a prick, checking you out when he has his girlfriend with him. "

Do you understand how both the girls' past experiences really changed the way the event was perceived and the meanings that were given to it? Even more than that, do you notice that the emotional experience had by both the girls was totally different? I trust you can see how an individuals' emotional experience will also change a person's perception of a situation as well.

Exercise: You can only have that which you can language

So first, you need to be aware of this and have an awareness of what you don't want in your life and what you do want. This can be in all areas of your life, intimate relationship, family relationships, career, financial wealth, hobbies and adventures, spirituality, health and vitality, relationship with self and life purpose. Get curious and inspired to look at things you never thought were even possible. Everything is impossible until it is possible or as Nelson Mandela said, "It always seems impossible until it is done."

Take the time to score each of these areas between 0 and 10. With 0 being completely unsatisfied and 10 being completely satisfied. Then write a list of what you don't want in an intimate relationship, and then, on a separate piece of paper, write what you do want. To know what we want, we must first know what we don't want. After you have done this for every section in your life, have a clearing ceremony where you burn the lists of what you don't want. Keep the lists of what you do want on a vision board or in a special place where you will see them every day.

Now that you have created the possibilities of what you actually want in life (remember these are also ever changing, so be adaptive), we can now get into creating awareness around what is actually there for you to release, to open your heart up to love and step into your power.

Take time to fall back in love with yourself

Date yourself! Take time with yourself, to love your thoughts and feelings, and spending time in your own company. Take the time to reconnect with yourself, take yourself out on adventures. Experience the world around you and what life has for you. Ask yourself each time you experience something new, "Do I actually like this?, or is it something someone else told me I should like? " The aim here is to get a definitive yes or no. To become more decisive and consciously know yourself better. It's ok if you don't actually like it. Great! You now know something you don't like. Now this is really important for later being able to find your voice, speak up and communicate boundaries, once you have opened your heart. You can't communicate something that you don't know!

Understanding ourselves and what we like and dislike can be a journey in itself. We grow up absorbing what our parents value, believe and like. We take on roles to fit into our tribe, so we can find our spot and belong. This is a biological survival behaviour pattern we all do. It comes from evolution of needing to have the safety of our tribe, because back in the stone age, if we got kicked out of our tribe, we would be eaten by the sabre-tooth tiger. We need to belong, it's a survival instinct!

We learn to belong and fit into our tribe through the roles we take on. Roles are behaviour patterns like being a people pleaser, a rescuer, a caretaker or peacekeeper, the warrior or hero, the good girl, the victim or designated patient, the rebel or scapegoat. Each of these roles work together; for example, if mum has a strong caretaker or rescuer role, she will need a victim or designated patient for her to rescue. So often a child will take that role on, to keep the peace and balance within the tribe. Humans are always reaching for homeostasis (balance), even if it means in an unhealthy way.

Each role we take on, has healthy and unhealthy parts of itself. For example, I am a recovering people pleaser. So my journey has been to identify the parts that don't serve me, and stop doing them. It takes awareness of when you are doing an action to make someone else happy, but it actually doesn't make you happy, crosses your boundaries and values and builds resentment within yourself towards the other person. The issue is, however, it came from not speaking up and communicating your boundary. The journey is to resign from the unresourceful parts of your roles, and of course keep the beautiful loving, gentle, useful, giving parts of it. You know when qualities of a role become unhealthy or unresourceful, when it is at the detriment of self, when your own needs are no longer being met. If you're needs aren't being met, chances are you are playing a role!

This is why the exercise above where you are articulating what you want and don't want is really important. We don't know what we don't know; and what you can't language, you are less likely to achieve.

Exercise: Make a list of the Roles you play in your life

Reflect on the roles mentioned above, create your own definition of what these look like in your life, and which 5 do you most strongly resonate with. For each one, write down the beautiful qualities in one column, and in another column the qualities that aren't in your best interest and don't nurture you. Now come up with some questions you could ask yourself when you notice the unresourceful traits showing up in everyday life of each trait. For eg. How is this serving me right now? Is this what I want or what someone else wants? For what purpose am I doing this action?

Do you have a gratitude practice?

I was having a chat with my uncle, who is a spiritual healer. I said I would like to improve my outward expression of gratitude, like him and his wife. They were openly grateful for everything they had, and it sometimes even made me feel uncomfortable. We started talking about ways I could show gratitude in my life and saying out loud a few things I was grateful for. Starting with simple things like running clean water, shelter over my head, and my beautiful kids. This then flowed into a session of experiencing love and companionship with the divine creator. Throughout this session, I realised I had an energetic barrier around my heart, like a leather guard I could visualize and feel. Experiencing gratitude is difficult if you have walls up around experiencing love and happiness from fear of getting hurt or loosing.

Bringing in gratitude into your life every day helps to reconnect with the love that is within you that is being trapped within from fear.

What are 3 things right now, that you are grateful for in your life?

Start your gratitude practice small if you find this hard to do, and gradually build to bigger statements and experiences of gratitude. Start each day, before you even get out of bed feeling the gratitude for 3 things in your life, it can be as small or big as you want. From the blanket you have keeping you warm while you slept, running water or the life you are designing. Take a moment to feel in your body, the appreciation and love for those things. It is the first step to opening up your heart.

Another exercise I love to do with my family around the dinner table which has really shunted the attitudes in my household is our "gratitudes" at dinner time. A few years ago, my beautiful friend Amanda was doing this in her family which I thought was so beautiful, and brought the family together. I have just added the last step on. My kids went from bickering, nitpicking and so critical towards each other, to a couple years later, looking after each other, working together and even at times singing together. This took about a month of me being consistent in enforcing it every night, and patiently waiting until they could answer in a nice way. It also creates positive conversation at the dinner table.

Exercise

We go around the table and each person gets their turn to answer the questions.

The questions are:

1. Best part of your day?
2. Something you're grateful for today?
3. Something nice about each person at the table?
4. Something you're proud of yourself for doing today?

Why do we build walls around our heart?

The heart chakra is one that is sacred and if blocked or closed will affect how you connect with other people in any relationship and is the gateway to connection with the universe. Your connection may be guarded, and reserved, or maybe the opposite, too open and vulnerable, leaving you open for others to take advantage of you, which leaves you going into victim and blame mode. Neither is resourceful nor going to help you ignite your power and the Goddess within. This is where the heart and throat chakra need to come together to ignite the empowerment and communication that a Goddess embodies. A Goddess no longer lets the past hold them back or shrinks in the grief, hurt or fear. A person who has a very guarded heart has been through a lot of pain and grief in their life. We are all human, and connection is a core human need. Connection, both physically and emotionally in life, is important to help a person thrive. When we have experienced grief, rejection, abandonment, and been hurt as a result; the fear of not being good enough or worthy can be triggered, which will manifest as walls around the heart.

When you think about a baby, they are born as their unique, centred self, in their purest form. They are the demonstration of universal truths that they are lovable; they are worthy and they are enough. What happens throughout human development and human nature, these truths turn into fears. A fear of not being lovable, not being worthy and not being good enough. This is because we are survival beings. We are animals who need to survive, and for us to survive, we need our tribe; we need connection. This survival instinct and primal mechanism is still in our brain, and it gets triggered every time we experience rejection, abandonment or loss.

It is for this reason that the fear of rejection is a major cause for people to start putting walls up around their heart. Unless you are doing the personal growth work, understanding your subconscious imprinting and releasing the behaviour patterns that have been passed on to you in your childhood, most people will be living from a place of fear.

Doesn't that sound like a prison to live in?

Now imagine you were actually walking around experiencing this fear of rejection every day, fear of being abandoned or rejected from your parents and tribe, rejected by the person you have a crush on, or being left out by your friends.

Do these sound like common issues a teenager experiences?

I know I remember being concerned with this as a teenager, and now I see my kids experience it too, and unless we take the conscious self love journey, we stay vibrating at the frequency of fear. The trick is to have your safety zone, people and an environment which allows you to feel safe, and loved in your whole state, the dark and the light bits of you. While yes, a parent can give you that unconditional love for all your dark and light bits of yourself which is a healthy foundation to thrive in life, as an adult, the real work has to start with you loving the dark and light bits of yourself. So how do we do that?

It's through our journey of falling back in love with ourselves, loving the thoughts that go through our mind, loving the deep and dark emotions that you experience, and being ok to show them to the people you want to really know you, and those people knowing how to receive them. This is why one of the first steps is dating yourself, and going on adventures by yourself. Experience the world around you, work out what you like and don't like, enjoy your own thoughts. If you don't enjoy, know and love these bits of yourself, how will anyone else truly know, love and enjoy these bits of you too?

When you love the deep and dark emotions, it means you no longer reject them- and reject that part of yourself. All our emotions, the dark and light, are a beautiful part of ourselves that are sending us messages to help us grow and evolve. What happens through human development, when those universal truths turn to fears, is that we are starting to reject the bits of ourselves, that we fear will be rejected. It's the need for survival within us that when we get shamed for doing something, it triggers the fear of rejection and being kicked out of the tribe.

If our mother operated from her own fear of loss as we grew up and didn't like us taking risks, being playful or being spontaneous, because she felt it was unsafe and she couldn't control the risks, our fear of our mother rejecting us would have been triggered if we were too risky. This threatens our survival, so we as that child, we play it safe, we stop taking risks, being spontaneous and playful. We think we need to be controlled and serious like the adults in our lives. We reject the centred self traits of being spontaneous, playful and taking risks, that help children develop courage and certainty in their own ability. Being spontaneous and taking risks helps a child develop calmness, trust in self and confidence in being able to embrace the uncertainty of life. The life journey is one of returning to your centred self that you were born as, and reigniting that curious and creative playfulness, along with the spontaneity and risk taking to increase courage, confidence and calmness in self.

How can you increase your curiosity in the world around you and develop playfulness, spontaneity and the ability to take risks and thus belief in self?

Exercise
Take some time now to brainstorm and commit to at least one thing each week, that you can do that embodies playfulness, adventure, spontaneity, and taking a risk, stepping out of your comfort zone. It could be as simple as jumping in a puddle when it's raining, turning the music up and dancing, going for a walk through your local forest, play with your kids, be silly, messy, paint a picture, have a swing in the park. Whatever resonates with you and is something you once loved to do.

Consciously give and receive love!

As life continues and we haven't started acknowledging this natural human fear of rejection, we subconsciously continue to put walls up around our heart to protect us from getting hurt, rejected or abandoned. Focusing on how you can bring more warmth and love to your conversations and relationships in your life is important. When you think of a baby, they are just love, and expect that they are loved. They have an innate warmth towards others. This is where we want to get back to. This is the mindset work that will help you be your centred self with compassion for self and others, authentically connected to others in their environment, and have clarity and confidence in where you stand in relationships.

So how do we nurture this connectivity, compassion, warmth and love?

Humans can be fantastic at giving to others, sometimes at the detriment of ourselves; but so often we aren't taught to receive from others, unless we're in victim role, and how to give to ourselves first. To receive love, we need to feel safe with those around us.

"We are the sum of the 5 people we spend the most time with." (Jim Rohn)

If we are surrounded by people who are defensive, argumentative, emotionally reactive and never listen to another's point of view, we are going to find it hard to feel deeply safe in our environment. If the people we surround ourselves with are always telling us what to do and not gently guiding us to find our own solutions and make our own mistakes, we can feel judged, sometimes controlled, and not good enough.

To feel safe, and empowered within ourselves we need to feel loved even in our messy. When we have a value of growth and improvement, and we are surrounded by people who love us in our messy, it will only inspire us to want to keep improving in our lives. I would also recommend going to women's healing, connection circles, and immersing yourself in environments that are about giving and receiving love.

As the recovering good girl, who particularly loved to please and conform to what my dad thought was right, I was unresourcefully rebelling against my dad, and my ex-husband, in messy ways, whether it be messiness in the house, or being late. These really annoy my dad particularly. I kept pushing to be loved by them in my messy, rather than judged and told you're not doing a good enough job, and I failed again. This is a really unhealthy cycle that I lived for a very long time. But my subconscious that was driving my behaviour was screaming "Just love and accept me for who I am!"

Be ok to sit with me and have a coffee in the middle of my mess, because I needed to be seen for me, not the environment around me.

When I tell this story to parents who I am coaching, they argue back that they are "just trying to help". Yes, of course, however there is a way to help that is empowering, and a way that becomes rescuing and disempowering. Helping to encourage those around us and also ask ourselves, "What do you/ I need?" helps to empower the person to communicate their needs. This is crucial to live an authentic, empowered life!

The result from helping someone when they have asked for it, comes with it a much deeper appreciation and gratitude, because they were ready to receive the help and gift.

Reflection

Take some time to reflect on how you reject your parents love? Do you sometimes push back on their expression of love?

Focus on giving these to yourself first

To grow and develop with our self-esteem intact, we have three aspects that needed to be met by our caregivers. Sharon Pearson calls it our self-esteem triad. We need our physical needs to be met, our emotions to be validated and accepted and our boundaries respected. This also helps us feel safe. The feeling of safety is hard to be measured however it is so crucial in keeping all our chakras open, and directly related to the heart as well.

Physical needs are usually a given- the need for shelter, safety not harm, food, clothing and warmth.

Were your boundaries respected as a child?

Respecting children's boundaries has not been a common part of raising children in the past. As society moves out of the patriarchal family design, where kids weren't allowed to say no to their parents, or have an opinion, it does not surprise me that domestic violence is such an issue in society. If a person has always been told they are not allowed to talk back, speak up, say I'm not hungry, or say no to their caregivers, as it is not respectful, why would they start saying no in their intimate relationships as a teenager or adult? It takes time and awareness to understand your own boundaries including what you like and what you don't like. This is why the first step of being connected to self by experiencing life and going on adventures is so important to understand yourself better. How can you say no, or set a boundary if you actually don't know what you like? You can't.

The third part of the triad is having your emotions accepted and validated. On this journey of opening your heart to ignite the Goddess within, increasing emotional intelligence is crucial.

In general, society doesn't accept the darker emotions. We are taught that it's not ok to have anger, to be sad or to be frustrated. If we do express these, we might get kicked out of our tribe, because they are not accepted and people don't know how to hold space for another when they are experiencing these emotions.

The first key belief, and often hardest, that needs to be wrestled with is that **"anger is a normal healthy human emotion when expressed resourcefully"**, where property or people are not being damaged or hurt in the process. What happens, however, is because we are taught it is not ok to experience anger, we suppress it. Our mind fights internally between "I am feeling anger", and "no, you shouldn't be angry". So we don't accept it and allow it to be released in a healthy way. So we end up having anger simmering underneath the surface until either the bucket overflows, or there are just too many triggers that cause you to explode. This explosion is aggression, and aggression is not ok. Learning to acknowledge, accept, own, feel and release anger, in a healthy way, is so important in reconnecting with self. When you can love and respect your own anger, and actually be grateful for the emotion of anger; because it is communicating something to you, you will reconnect and love a part of yourself that has been rejected for so long.

This reconnection experience with self is life changing!

When we don't allow ourselves to have emotions, we trap the emotional energy within us. The word emotion comes from the Latin word, 'emotere', which means 'energy in motion'. Emotions have now been measured scientifically by Hawkins and can be found in the Hawkins scale of emotional frequency. Emotions are just energy, so we need to learn to release the energy. It's the meanings we put to the emotional experience that keep hurting us. This is why I often recommend to people to combine this conscious mindset work with energetic healing as well, for example working with a Reiki master to help as well. They work beautifully and holistically together. So become aware of the thoughts you are having about an emotional experience and what are you making it mean. What story are you telling yourself about it?

If you notice there is story, check in with the person to actually see if your story and meaning is accurate. Often we make up the worse case scenario and meaning about a situation without finding out the facts, and it keeps hurting our soul.

Becoming emotionally intimate with self is the journey to reconnecting with your heart chakra. So often, humans can just be going through the motions and not consciously thinking about their direction and purpose in life. I have found that grief, fear, abandonment or loss are often the underlying emotions underneath anger. Once you are able to experience anger resourcefully, the other heavy emotions can be processed and released resourcefully as well. We notice anger more easily because it has more external signs. However, something like hurt or grief have quieter signs and rarely get the respect and acknowledgement they deserve. For example, if you're grieving the death of a baby or even a relationship, often the response from loved ones around you is to 'move on', 'keep yourself busy', 'be the warrior', 'you'll be ok'. These responses are, of course, coming from love and wanting to stop you from experiencing the darker emotions. However, darker emotions are part of the human experience. I once had an aunty, who had suffered a great loss tell me that she just keeps praying for her anger to be taken away. My response to this was, "if you are asking for you not to have anger, you are asking to not have the human experience. Don't ask for it to be taken away. Ask for the tools to be able to process it and release it, so then you can teach your daughter how to do the same." When you allow yourself to experience all your deeper and darker emotions, connection to your centred self increases. Your courage and confidence that you can handle anything that comes your way increases. Your trust in self increases. You soon realise that emotions come and go, and you are still ok. They are not something to fear, you are still whole, ok, and loved even when you do have them!

Having people in your life that can first give love to you while you are experiencing the darker emotions is the most powerful experience and the gateway to loving them yourself. I remember the first time I had a coach hold space for me, while I fell apart because of a heart break I experienced, someone who I now understand is a soul mate, was unable to be the person I wanted him to be for me. The hurt and rejection was deep. As deep as I have ever felt. My coach was just there for me, witnessing me and still pouring on the love me, even when I was hurting, and being a little irrational by putting meanings on the rejection I experienced as I was not good enough, deep to my core. He heard me, he validated me and made my heart ache feel understood and seen, the loneliness and rejection I felt was no longer as extreme and painful. I was still accepted in my messy. It was mind blowing! A new benchmark of how I wanted my intimate partner to be able to show me love. This is what everyone deserves in their relationships, if they choose it to be important, and they want to be seen in their wholeness.

To open your heart chakra, live to experience more joy in your life, and start with consciously bringing gratitude practices into your life. Surround yourself with people who are living consciously and know how to give real love, not love that is ego based. Create awareness of where you reject receiving love and give yourself permission to receive.

Do the work to love and connect with yourself, and love all your shadows. To allow yourself to connect to your heart, it is necessary to get intimate with your emotions. Feel those emotions that end up blocking your heart. It is important to process and release feeling hurt, grief, abandonment, loss, rejection, heart break, hatred, feeling offended, disappointed, let down, disillusioned, vulnerable or neglected. These are all emotions that are connected to the heart chakra, and the walls we build around it that are necessary to be attended to and released. If you are able to connect with what each of these emotions feels like and let them go, you are well on your way to emotional intelligence and living your authentic life with an open heart!

Reflection

Write down key take aways and steps you can see you need to take in your life to open and keep open your heart chakra!

Resources:

To access the resources mentioned in this book go to
https://reclaimyourinnergoddess.com.au/resources

Even If Your Voice Shakes...

with Margie McCumstie

"Stand before the people you fear and speak your mind - even if your voice shakes." These words were declared by a woman named Maggie Kuhn. Maggie was forced to retire when she reached 65 and by joining together with other elderly people, created a revolution called the "Grey Panthers" in America to ensure that older people had a voice. She led nursing home reform, ended forced retirement and ensured that older citizens were respected as part of the community with opinions about social issues and able to make a difference.

Maggie's passion for her cause and her ability to speak- despite the fear, allowed her to be successful in making a contribution. Did Maggie have extraordinary courage or unique skills? Was Maggie an incredibly confident woman, immune to criticism?

I suspect not.

Maggie had passion and conviction and the willingness to make a stand for herself and others. And I imagine she had great personal boundaries.

Without strong boundaries, you are open to others encroaching on your power and to having your communication hindered. Maggie says to stand before the people you fear- but to be able to do that, you must first face the person who is most likely to silence your voice.

That person is you.

I used to hate the concept of boundaries. I always felt they were cold and just a way of distancing ourselves from others, but then I heard Lola Pickett say in her "Empath to Power" podcast that "to not have boundaries was to allow unkindness to thrive". This idea floored me. Being a people pleaser from way back, I was willing to allow my lack of boundaries to allow unkindness to me.

I decided to actively explore the concept of boundaries in my life and as soon as I had opened the door, the universe brought me opportunities to assert them.

Five months earlier, a woman in a group on Facebook had posted that she was suicidal and alone. I reached out to her immediately and it wasn't long before we were talking. She started leaning on me very heavily and we spoke for many hours as she poured out her heart and told me about her life as a trans woman, rejected by her family and struggling to get by on her pension. She wasn't eating properly and was often emotional. I begged her to seek help but she felt those doors had been closed to her and preferred to just rely on me. I bought her groceries and sent her gifts to cheer her up. I tried to get her to focus on gratitude. I listened and gently guided her away from suicidal thoughts and helped her as best I could. When she asked me after a couple of weeks of talking if she could be my sister, I agreed. I organised for my Mum to talk to her and to take on forming a Mother/Daughter relationship. When she shared her distress at spending another Christmas alone, I invited her to come up and share Christmas with our family. Our family Christmases were fairly closed, intimate gatherings but I asked my family to open their hearts and homes to have her join us. I paid for her flights and offered to send her money so she could buy gifts. She said that she wouldn't know what to buy and that she would rather just receive. She came to stay and the intense rollercoaster of talks, crying and anger began. It was tumultuous and exhausting. She was accepted by everyone, showered with thoughtful gifts and treated very well. We wanted her to feel welcome and comfortable so we covered all her expenses and went out of our way to do things that she would enjoy. But there were times where she would bang her head against the wall, cry in the foetal position or talk about killing herself. During her visit, my cousin unexpectedly died and I was upset and shocked. My focus left her. She became distressed that I wasn't making her the priority and so I shelved my grief and returned my focus to her. Once she returned home, I received an email saying that nothing I could do or say would ever make a difference to her. I felt frustrated that all my immense efforts had seemingly been for nothing. There was no gratitude, no appreciation and I felt depleted, exhausted and completely used up.

After she returned home, my grief for my cousin had returned and as I'm a Celebrant, I needed to prepare to perform her funeral. I wrote to my friend and asked for a little space to give me a chance to find my feet. We had a conversation where I asked her to explore with a professional if there was a possibility she had borderline personality disorder. She confirmed that she had been diagnosed with it previously and I saw how manipulative she had been over the months. It had reached the point of desperation for me and so I asked that she take some time to seek some professional help as I wasn't capable of being her only source of assistance. It was my first time asserting a boundary with her and for myself. It was met with rage and fury. Accusations, insults and nasty communication came in a barrage. I wrote to her again and made sure my communication was very clear. I was compassionate but clear. I told her that how she was treating me was unacceptable and that I would be willing to speak to her again once she had sought some professional help. However, the communication continued and it became increasingly obvious that her mental illness was in full swing. I knew the communication didn't reflect who she really was, so I asked her not to contact me until she was working on her recovery and not for three months in the first instance. This was unacceptable to her and she made threats towards me. I told her that I would take any future threats to the police and seek a restraining order if necessary and asked her to please seek professional help. At this point, she ended our friendship in an aggressive and nasty manner.

And whilst it is sad that things have turned out like they have, I am also peaceful. I refused to treat her like a victim or allow myself to continue being a martyr. I set boundaries and stayed strong. I was fearful of doing so because I didn't want to hurt her but to not do so, would be to allow myself to continue being used and hurt. Lola was right, not having boundaries allows unkindness to thrive.

So many of us, especially women, have been taught from a young age to be people pleasers. People pleasing can also be a means of survival. The problem with people pleasing is that the "people" this refers to is a group that does not include you. When your needs and desires are barely considered, personal boundaries are eroded and you lose your voice. Vishuddha is the throat chakra and a block in the energy of this chakra compromises our access to communicate freely, to express ourselves and ultimately to be able to speak freely and openly. When we do not give personal priority to boundaries or allow others to encroach them, we allow our throat chakras to become blocked and we lose not just our voice, but our personal power as well. We can claim it back, freeing our voice and reclaiming our power by observing our relationships with boundaries.

Do you lack personal boundaries?

10 signs you lack personal boundaries
1. You fail to speak up when mistreated.
2. You prioritise yourself last or not at all.
3. You allow others to take advantage of you.
4. You give away your time, energy and resources.
5. You agree (or stay silent) when you actually feel like disagreeing.
6. You feel guilty for dedicating time for yourself.
7. You feel like a victim or a martyr.
8. You are prone to burnout and exhaustion.
9. Your worth is dependent on connection.
10. You use words like "helpful", "selfless" and "compassionate" to justify your existence.

It is important to recognise that if you see yourself in this list of traits as I did that you do not have to stay there. It is also important to realise that not only do you have the power to change, but you also have the power to offer yourself compassion as you consciously create or re-establish boundaries.

If we flip my 10 signs you lack boundaries, we discover a loving roadmap to being able to create boundaries, use our voice (even if it shakes) and to reclaim our inner goddess.

The 10 signs you are powerful with boundaries

1. You know your worth and do not allow yourself to be mistreated.
2. You prioritise yourself in your own life.
3. You are clear with others about your boundaries to ensure you are content with your contribution.
4. You are mindfully generous with your time, energy and resources within the boundaries that work for you.
5. You express your disagreement if it is safe to do so and remove yourself if it is not.
6. You actively seek and cherish dedicated time for yourself.
7. You recognise the strength and personal power of living with integrity and accountability.
8. You are able to say yes joyfully and to say no without guilt.
9. Your worth is intrinsically linked to your humanity and you are a wondrous, magnificent being.
10. You have many valuable traits but do not need them to justify your existence. You recognise that not being "selfless" does not make you "selfish".

Creating a new paradigm for your life in relation to boundaries, worth and communication is exciting, daunting, empowering and possibly scary. So, let's explore each of the ten signs and examine what they look like in practice. And that is what it is- a practice. You won't always get it perfect but it will grow stronger and easier as you flex the muscle.

1. You know your worth and do not allow yourself to be mistreated

You'll notice that in my interaction with my friend, I allowed myself to be mistreated over time and it was only when I reached breaking point that I realised that it was going on. This can be bypassed by meditation, journaling and going inward to check in with how you are feeling. I hadn't set boundaries within myself so it was easy for me to be mistreated.

Knowing your worth as an individual and as a friend is important to ensuring that you can define boundaries that preserve and protect your worth. There will always be layers as well. For example, a friend of mine was in a toxic relationship with her husband where he was emotionally abusive but when the abuse became physical, she drew a line in the sand as to what was acceptable and left him. After that relationship, she realised that emotional abuse was also not okay and a new boundary was created. After a few occasions of asserting that boundary with new partners, she is now settled in a happy relationship.

Boundaries can be created in any situation, including work. In work situations, this can be negotiated but can also mean that you may need to be prepared to leave your work situation. Sometimes the boundary extends beyond mistreatment of yourself as an individual to mistreatment of a coworker, customer or client which doesn't align with your values.

For example, many years ago, I used to be an Early Childhood Teacher and started a role as a Teaching Director at a child care centre. On my first day, I noticed many things that were not reflecting a high quality standard. In fact, there were many aspects that weren't even meeting a basic standard. These were things I felt I could change in my role as the Centre Director.

Then I met Crystal. Crystal was a four year old girl with big eyes and a mischievous spirit. Within hours of meeting Crystal, I had observed some very troubling behaviours- representational drawings of people standing around and someone lying on top of a smaller person she identified as her. The other people were "Mummy's friends". In the bathroom, she fingered herself. In the home play area, she acted out having sex with the dolls. I documented everything in detail and the staff asked how I was finding Crystal. I asked if any reports had been made to child protective services and what had previously been observed. I was directed to a large file of observations and accounts by other staff. I read through them in horror and again asked if reports had been made. The answer was simply "No, the owners said not to, because Crystal comes five days a week and her younger sister will be starting here next year and will also be coming five days a week, so it is worth too much to them." This was completely unacceptable to me and so I took the entire file with my most current observations, accounts and reports and visited the Department of Community Services and we met for a few hours. I resigned the following day. I was unwilling to stay in a position that required me to be complicit with abuse. It wasn't convenient to leave my new job but I'd rather leave with my ethics and integrity than stay with shame, guilt and fear.

2. You prioritise yourself in your own life

Women are known for putting others first and mothers are expected to put their families before themselves. But prioritising everyone ahead of yourself is clearly not working with the Australian Bureau of Statistics reporting in their 2018 National Health Survey that around 1 in 6 women in Australia will experience depression and 1 in 3 women will experience anxiety during their lifetime. They also found that women experience post-traumatic stress disorder and eating disorders at higher rates than men. When we prioritise ourselves, we live happier and more fulfilled lives and are better able to contribute to our relationships, families and communities. There is an old story that goes that the universe will first throw a grain of sand to get you to pay attention. Then a pebble will be thrown, then a stone, then a rock, then a boulder. When we prioritise others before ourselves all the time, we will often miss, ignore or deny the signs until the boulder almost crushes us. It is at that point when the mental health problems or physical health crisis hits that we are forced to prioritise ourselves.

That was certainly the case for me many years ago when I was in a workplace with a toxic workplace culture, unreasonable demands and unsupportive management structure. I held on despite this because I prioritised my job and my financial security. I ignored the signs until the boulder hit and I was crushed with depression and anxiety and had months off, seeking help and recovering. Phrases like "self-care" and "self-love" have become more prevalent in recent years as women are realising that the standard of "putting everyone first" is an unhelpful patriarchal construct.

3. You are clear with others about your boundaries to ensure you are content with your contribution

How often do we say "Yes" when we really mean "No"? Whether we say yes from a place of people pleasing, habit, resignation or controlling, when we do so, we are actually saying both yes and no. Yes to others but no to ourselves. No to our truth, our time, our families. When we recognise that there is a cost to saying yes, we can choose to put some personal boundaries in place to ensure that your yes is a real yes and does not become a resentful one. What does this look like? A good way to do this, especially when learning to flex the muscle, is to buy yourself some time to check in with what you want, need and deserve. Sometimes that might mean a response like "Thanks for the opportunity, I'll think about it and get back to you" or "I'll need to check my diary and see if I can make that work" or "I'm not sure, I'll let you know".

With practice, the self check in might only take a few seconds so you can say no. Or yes. But if it is yes, it can be given freely. To participate in doing something because you have genuinely chosen to say yes is freedom.

4. You are mindfully generous with your time, energy and resources within the boundaries that work for you

Having access to say no without guilt and yes without resentment is exciting, but I'm sure we have all been in situations when saying yes has blown into a bigger commitment than we anticipated. It is important to remember that even if the answer is yes, it can be given with an articulation of boundaries as well. This might require a response like "yes, I can do that but I'll need an extra week" or "yes, I'm happy to help if I can have more assistance/ bigger budget" or "yes, that sounds good as long as someone else can look after the (component you don't want to do)." Each time you do this, the ability to do so becomes stronger and you honour yourself.

It is never too late to establish a boundary even if one hadn't been set before. One way to do this is to voice how you are feeling, express what isn't working and what you need to move forward. An example of this would be to say "Hey team, I'm feeling really tired and stressed about our project. It isn't working for me anymore to be doing X/ working on Y/ coordinating Z, and if I could have some help with A and someone step up to look after Z, that would be helpful." Renegotiation says to yourself "I'm important" and says to the others involved "I need you to respect my boundaries". If the renegotiation fails, as it sometimes does in workplaces, then you'll need to consider what your "No" might look like.

5. You express your disagreement if it is safe to do so and remove yourself if it is not

I look back in admiration at my 15 year old self and the confidence she had one day. I attended a girl's catholic school in Sydney until Year 10 and we had one term of dancing each Friday with the boys from a local boy's school. We were doing a progressive ballroom dance and I could see a guy ahead who was refusing to hold his partner's hands and was leaving her to do the steps on her own with her hands up. The teachers weren't doing anything about it and I was angry that my classmates were being humiliated and that my turn was coming up. When I reached this boy, I said "You will hold my hands and dance properly" and he laughed at me. I told him that he needed to learn to be a gentleman and with that, I put my nose in the air and left the hall. I walked out and caught the train home and when I arrived home, my Mum was waiting and worried as the school had called. I told Mum what had happened and told her to tell the school that the supervision needed to ensure we were being treated appropriately. In this situation, I said what the girls before me felt they couldn't and when that didn't work, I removed myself. I held true to my convictions and when the school wanted to question my leaving the hall, I held firm and asked my Mum to back me and remind the school of their responsibilities.

Integrity is incredibly important and when your strongly held convictions are pushed against, it is vital that you speak your truth. Now, you might say that's possible at home, with family or with friends but in work situations, that it is impossible. Holding that as a belief makes you trapped at work, a victim to your boss and a slave to security. While I completely understand the need for job security, the cost is too great if it compromises your integrity. To give you an example, I was working as the Club Manager for a large gym and a young single mother joined the gym. After the first three months, her situation drastically changed and she struggled to pay her membership. I approached the owners and asked for leniency and asked for a special exemption to cancel her membership. They agreed but said she would have to give a month's notice and pay for that month. I told her of their decision and she missed the payment. Her membership was not cancelled then because she had money owing and she begged me in tears to help. I approached the owners again and asked if we could cancel the membership and let her pay the amount left and they refused and said that she would have to pay another month if she wanted to cancel and if she didn't pay that, they would send her to the debt collectors for the full membership amount. I phoned this member and explained the situation and she was extremely distressed. I offered to pay her membership fees so she could cancel and took the risk that she would pay me back. It was my personal choice to do this and I was willing to lose the money if I needed to. As I was completing the process, one of the owners walked in and saw me putting my card through the eftpos machine and questioned me. I didn't have anything to hide and told her what I had chosen to do. Within 24 hours, I had to have a formal meeting with both owners and had received a warning. I thought this was preposterous and told them so- they could not dictate how I spent my money! They said "we are not leaving this room until you promise never to use your money to pay for another member again" and as compassion is one of my core values, that was simply a promise I couldn't make. I had no intention of making it a regular occurrence, nor did I have the financial means to do so, but I could not promise them what they were asking. So I simply responded "I can't make that promise but I promise that I do understand that my job will be in jeopardy if I do". They both looked at me with disbelief and horror but they had met a firm boundary with me. I was willing to compromise and work extra hours or do things outside my job description but this was not negotiable for me. I'll always be proud of standing up for myself in this situation.

6. You actively seek and cherish dedicated time for yourself

A friend of mine is caring for her beautiful mother who is in her final stages of life. Although she is caring around the clock, she realises that without some boundaries in place for dedicated alone time and time with friends outside of the house, that she can't give fully to her Mum. Giving fully doesn't have to mean losing yourself and after my friend has caught up with girlfriends or come back from a swim, she has more energy to support her Mum and be present in these difficult and magical final weeks.

7. You recognise the strength and personal power of living with integrity and accountability

Tara Winkler saw a problem in Cambodia when she volunteered as a tourist at an orphanage and set about raising money to help the children and to return to make a difference. When she returned, she soon realised that the orphanage was corrupt and the children were not safe. So Tara rescued the children and started her own orphanage. As time went by and Tara's understanding grew, she realised that many of the children were not actually orphans at all and indeed, had family that didn't have the resources to raise their children. She saw that "voluntourism" was adding to the problems and created the Cambodian Children's Trust to work with communities, families and children to create change. This meant facing that she had unknowingly contributed to the issues. As they say "when you know better, you do better" and so even though the path of staying an orphanage may have been "easier" or more lucrative, Tara had the courage and integrity to stay true to her mission and accountable for her contribution. If you'd like to read more about Tara's amazing story or support her work, her book "How (not) to start an Orphange: By a woman who did" is insightful and inspiring.

8. You are able to say yes joyfully and to say no without guilt

We talked about this earlier and after consideration, a joyful yes probably seems more accessible than a no without guilt. We often feel like we have to give a reason or an excuse as to why we are saying no. The no could just be a no with no reason given. Often you may want to say more to justify your no so you don't seem unreasonable but this can be another form of people pleasing. The other reason you may choose to say more is so your no can't be eroded by the other person. When you accept that a considered "no" is also a "yes" to you, and you value yourself enough to honour that, there is nothing that can erode it and you will be able to stand strong. In 2019, I was doing some casual work for a national business and so when my Dad became sick, I told my employer that I wasn't available for shifts as I was caring for my Dad. My Dad died five weeks later and I was honoured to perform his funeral. I notified my workplace and told them I needed some time. A couple of weeks later, my employer contacted me and said that they wanted to roster me onto regular shifts. I thanked them but apologised that I was still deeply grieving and wasn't ready. I offered to do an occasional shift to help out but regular shifts weren't going to work for me as I was dealing with Dad's house and grief. They said I didn't have a choice and that if I didn't start doing regular shifts, they would have to let me go. I reminded them that I was a casual and that I did have a choice. We parted ways that day and I had zero regrets. I gave reasons, thinking they might show some understanding or compassion but my "no" was firm.

9. Your worth is intrinsically linked to your humanity and you are a wondrous, magnificent being

Sunitha Krishnan trained to be a social worker in India and as a young woman, started helping her community teach local children. A group of eight men decided that this young woman needed to be "put in her place" and gang raped her and beat her so badly that she became deaf in one ear.

In India, rape is a cause for shame and humiliation for the victim. But Sunitha was not going to allow this act by eight men to determine her worth and she knew she needed to stand strong and allow her light to shine. "I chose not to feel like a victim. I am not a victim. I am a survivor. I speak about it with a lot of pride, because I am proud of what I have become today. I have not done a mistake. I don't want my face to be blurred. I am not to be ashamed for. The guys that have done it should be hiding their faces and they should be blurring their faces" said Sunitha.

With a fierce commitment, Prajwala which means "eternal flame" was created. Sunitha knew there was a need in her community and wanted to make a difference. When you discover the statistics, the problem may seem very overwhelming but with conviction and integrity as core values, Sunitha was intent on ending sex slavery- and still is. The statistics are staggering- 18 million women and children are involved in sexual slavery in India alone. 200 thousand women and children are forced into prostitution each year and 65 thousand children are trafficked each year with some of these being as young as 5 years.

Undaunted by the enormity of the issue, Prajwala works on the five pillars of Prevention, Protection, Rescue, Rehabilitation and Reintegration. Through medical, psychological and legal support, women and children are given opportunities to heal and rebuild their lives. If Sunitha had allowed that gang rape to determine her worth, Prajwala would not be making the difference it does today. Learn more or support them further by visiting: https://www.prajwalaindia.com/.

10. You have many valuable traits but do not need them to justify your existence. You recognise that not being "selfless" does not make you "selfish"

We are facing a crisis that is escalating each year. The examples of the "ideal" that were once seen in magazines and television are now all pervasive when we add social media to the mix. We have more incidences of depression, anxiety and mental health issues than ever before as we compare ourselves against air-brushed, filter imposed or surgically enhanced images. And it isn't just "beauty ideals" that we compare against, it is also financial goals, measures of success and lifestyle achievements.

Sometimes we find our value in relation to our careers- but that is only part of who we are.

Sometimes we find our value in relation to our partner or family, like they make us more worthwhile. They are a special part of your life and might make your life feel more worthwhile but your worth is there regardless.

Sometimes we feel our worth as our role as Mum. Mums are loving, caring and selfless and so many women lose themselves in the "mum life". Being a Mum is undoubtedly worth treasuring, but is not all you are.

And so, if your role, career, relationships, weight, appearance, financial status, intelligence, personality or lifestyle do not make you more or less worthy of being on the planet, what does, then? Your very existence. You are a unique expression in the world, just by being here. You wouldn't argue that a person with a disability was a lesser person, so why would you consider that you would be for any reason? We each have talents and abilities that are special to us and from a base of inherent worthiness, we have the opportunity to use them to express ourselves in our lives.

We can each create the life we want to live and choose how that looks, seizing opportunities to prioritise ourselves and what is important to us. By using our voices as a means of self expression, we honour our individuality and passions. By using our voices to advocate for ourselves and others, we can make a difference in our world. Katy Perry sings about the transformation possible from unblocking your throat chakra and speaking your truth in her song, "Roar"- "I used to bite my tongue and hold my breath, Scared to rock the boat and make a mess, So I sat quietly, agreed politely. I guess that I forgot I had a choice, I let you push me past the breaking point, I stood for nothing, so I fell for everything. You held me down, but I got up,

Already brushing off the dust, You hear my voice, you hear that sound, Like thunder, gonna shake the ground… and you're gonna hear me roar" And Helen Reddy knew of the power women had when they joined their voices in unifying strength when she sang "I am Woman, hear me roar".

So, dearest reader, remember- you ARE strong, you ARE invincible, you ARE woman and you can reclaim your voice and your inner goddess.

You deserve it. X

Resources:

To access the resources mentioned in this book go to
https://reclaimyourinnergoddess.com.au/resources

Unlocking Your Inner Wisdom
- Intuitive Gift Activation

with Shari Ware

"Your inner self is wise beyond limits. You're tapped into the universal Source, which has access to all knowledge."
— Doreen Virtue

So you're working on reclaiming your inner goddess! That's exciting!

According to dictionary.com, the definition of a goddess is:
1. a female god or deity.
2. a woman of extraordinary beauty and charm.
3. a greatly admired or adored woman: a domestic goddess who hosts lavish dinner parties.

I actually think that's a pretty crappy definition and doesn't even begin to scratch the surface of what a true goddess is. I'm sure by this point in the book, you have a much better definition already, so tell me…... what are some of the attributes of a goddess? What do we mean when we say we want to "reclaim our inner goddess". It depends on who you're asking, doesn't it? It can mean many and varied things to each of us and so what's really important is, what does it mean to YOU?!

By this point, you should already have a fairly good grasp on what it DOES mean to you and if there is more refinement to be done, this chapter will help with that process. It's time to unlock your inner wisdom by activating your intuitive gifts!

Before we get into that though, I feel it's important for me to paint you a picture of what life can be like when we haven't yet learned to trust our inner knowing.

I used to be the size of a baby elephant. That wasn't a comparison I made. A tv reporter interviewing me made that "inspiring" comparison. In the few years prior to 2010, I was classed as severely morbidly obese. I actually don't know what my heaviest weight was, however I do know that it would have been well over 180 kilos. I started putting on weight around the age of 5. I didn't have the worst childhood in the world, however I did have a challenging one at times and emotional eating was a behaviour that manifested as a result. Between the ages of 6 and 8, I had a couple of instances of sexual abuse that further compounded the problem. I kept eating and by the time I finished high school, I was easily 100 kilos.

After I turned 18, I decided I might like to have a boyfriend, as I had never had one before. I didn't like what I saw in the mirror though and in my mind, if I didn't like the picture I presented to the world, then how could anyone else? So I embarked on a mission to lose weight and lost about 40 kilos, getting down to a size 12. I did meet a lovely young man and we ended up in a relationship together and within a couple of years, we had a baby daughter.

We were young, with a new baby and there was a lot of stress on the relationship. I also had a lot of self-esteem and emotional issues because of my childhood that I didn't realise I hadn't actually dealt with. It was the perfect recipe for a roller coaster relationship that was on and off over a 9-year period until it finally ended. My weight had also been a roller coaster over the period of the relationship and by the time we made our final goodbyes, I was well over 140 kilos.

In the years directly after the relationship ended, I continued to gain weight and was in a very dark place emotionally. What I didn't know for a long time and finally realised in the end, is that my weight was actually a physical suit of armour. I created it to protect myself. I had been very hurt when my relationship ended and I didn't want to repeat that, so subconsciously, I decided that I needed to make myself so unattractive to the opposite sex that I didn't have to worry about anyone ever asking me out and it worked very well!

I did finally become aware of what I was doing, but because the fear was still there subconsciously, I wasn't able to do anything about the weight, no matter how hard I tried. And I tried many, many times. Thankfully, one day I woke up and thought that maybe… just maybe… I might be ready to have a relationship again. My daughter was about 16 at the time and I realised that if I was lucky enough to still be alive (the fear of having a heart attack was ever present in my mind), then after she turned 18, I was going to be alone, on the couch with no life and that didn't seem like much fun to me. That was the switch that finally flipped and I was able to make changes to my lifestyle, one at a time, to release 100 kilos, changing my life forever.

The need for protection is the key element here. It caused me to create a dysfunctional physical protective shield around myself, which impacted my entire life in a very negative way and at the very core of it was the fact that I didn't trust myself. I didn't trust my inner voice… my inner knowing. I didn't trust that I could keep myself safe and so the weight was my way of achieving that outcome. It was a vicious cycle that kept continuing until the day I didn't feel the need for that protection anymore.

Luckily, a massive part of my weight release journey was personal development work, which continues to this day. This has helped me to learn to trust myself. To listen to that inner voice. To understand that I have everything inside of me I need. To believe in me. To know that I'm protected and safe.

If this resonates with you. If you've created a dysfunctional physical or energetic suit of armour around yourself and you're ready to let it go, I've created a beautiful process that will help you do just that, which I will take you through a little later on. For now, though, let's talk about where our inner wisdom comes from.

Let me introduce the Ajna, also known as The Sixth Chakra, Brow Chakra, Third Eye Chakra, Dragon Eye or Unicorn Horn - the gateway to your inner wisdom. Ajna is Sanskrit and its translation is "knowledge". The colour of the brow chakra is dark blue or indigo and it's the energy centre of our body which is responsible for intuition, spiritual awareness, reality, inner peace, perception, wisdom, thought and manifesting. It's situated at the bridge of the nose between the eyebrows and is associated with the pineal gland in the brain. The symbol for Ajna is a two-petalled rosette with a triangle pointing downwards inside a circle in the centre. The element of the brow chakra is light and the goddess who rules over the third eye chakra is Hakini Shakti, a goddess who has six heads and is representative of perfected meditation.

The organs connected to the third eye chakra include the nose, eyes, ears, nervous system and brain. The third eye chakra also governs the way the pineal gland and pituitary gland function. The pineal gland is situated deep within the centre of the brain in the epithalamus, is about the size of a grain of rice and is the shape of a small pine cone. It's part of the endocrine system and helps with regulating melatonin. The pineal gland produces melatonin, which controls our reproductive hormones and our sleep/wake cycle, known as our circadian rhythms. The pineal gland affects both our sexual maturation and our sleep patterns. The amount of melatonin released within our bodies has an effect on our stress levels and our resilience. Therefore, a balanced or imbalanced pineal gland will have a direct effect on our happiness and well-being. Excess mineral deposits and fluoride often cause the pineal gland to calcify, which may have an effect on sleep. The pineal gland produces less melatonin during the day because of its photosensitivity and more at night, thus explaining why most people are awake during the daytime and ready for sleep at night. Alternatively, the pituitary gland can be found in the brain in the hypothalamus, which also plays a role in our sleeping and waking schedule. It's like a master gland, controlling how many of the hormones in the body function. Therefore, proper functioning of the body requires the pineal gland and the pituitary gland to work together. When these glands are out of balance, it can cause serious problems with sleep and our wake/sleep cycle.

The element associated with the sixth chakra is the element of light, which can assist us in clearing and balancing our brow chakra. It makes sense, doesn't it? We're looking for enlightenment. We're looking for answers and clarity. Opening the third eye helps us to shine a light on parts of our life that may have been previously hidden in the dark. Elements that we were possibly unaware of. Awareness helps to bring so much clarity. This is the purpose of a healthy, balanced sixth chakra.

Not only do the chakras exist in the body, they also exist on our planet. What I find really interesting is that the third eye chakra doesn't have a permanent location on earth, shifting in conjunction with the earth's rotational axis and/or the constellations. The earth's third eye chakra is also known as the Aeon Activation Centre, which aligns with the belief that its location changes with each new astrological age or aeon. We are currently in the Age of Aquarius with the earth's third eye chakra lying in England at Glastonbury with the heart chakra. When we move into the Age of Capricorn, the location of the earth's third eye chakra is predicted to move to Brazil. This will occur somewhere around 3500 to 4600AD.

The Ajna allows us to see through "reality" to the underlying truth. It's what you may know as your "sixth sense", second sight or extrasensory perception, also known as ESP. The purpose of the third eye chakra is to allow us to see clearly and is responsible for our higher thoughts. Through the third eye, duality is dissolved and there is no longer the differentiation of "I" and "You" or "good" and "bad". When we have a balanced, clean brow chakra, we are blessed with strong insight and intuition. We also have clarity, strong emotional balance and self-awareness. A balanced and well-functioning third eye allows us to detach from emotion, enabling us to reach a higher understanding and a deeper knowledge.

On the flip side, when our third eye chakra is unbalanced or blocked, we may suffer from issues such as difficulty learning and concentrating, headaches, problems with the nervous system, mental confusion, lack of focus, hearing or eyesight problems. When the brow chakra is unbalanced, we may lack direction and struggle to find meaning in our lives. Often when we have a blocked sixth chakra, we find it difficult to be accepting of opinions or ideas that oppose our own and struggle to assume responsibility. We may feel unable to tap into our intuition and find that our imagination is lacking. Another manifestation of a blocked or unbalanced Ajna is depression, anxiety and being oppressed by fears which largely come about from our detachment from our true selves.

How does this come about? Most often, it goes back to our early years. If you were raised in an environment where you didn't feel as if you could speak your truth, then you will most likely have an unbalanced brow chakra. If, like me, you had a childhood that wasn't always emotionally stable, then you may also find you struggle with an unbalanced sixth chakra. Do you come from a culture or family where you were made to do what you were told without question? Did you feel oppressed in some way? Did you feel as if your opinion was valued? All of these scenarios contribute to a blocked third eye. For most of my life, I didn't feel as if I could speak my truth or as if what I thought, was important and that affected my physical and mental health in ways that I never imagined.

So, how healthy is your brow chakra? Is your brow chakra unbalanced or blocked? If you're not sure, ask yourself if any of the following apply to you:

- You're stubborn
- You get lost in your own world
- You can't connect to your higher self
- You struggle to find inspiration or creativity
- You're mistrustful or find it easy to dislike people
- You struggle to have an open mind
- You frequently suffer from migraines or headaches
- You don't listen to your intuition
- You're indecisive and unfocused
- You have problems with your eyesight and sinuses
- You regularly avoid reality via daydreaming
- You're easily upset and very emotional
- You have a strong attachment to outcomes
- You focus more on the details and struggle to see the overall picture
- You look outside yourself for happiness
- You give the perception of being opinionated and arrogant or ungrounded and dreamy

- You're excessively emotional or logical
- You interact with other people in a very superficial or trivial way
- You're not open to changing your opinions
- You struggle with mental health issues
- You don't have a clear grasp on reality

If several of the above apply to you, then your third eye chakra could definitely benefit from some healing and you've actually already taken the first step... awareness.

How does life change when you have a balanced and healthy third eye? I know for me; I had many beliefs that I didn't want to let go. Consciously, I thought I was open-minded, flexible and open to change and I realised looking back that I actually wasn't. A few years ago now, I remember distinctly attending a seminar on health and it totally blowing my mind. Up to that point, I had about 43 years of pretty ingrained beliefs around food and during that one 3 hour seminar they were blown to smithereens! Luckily, I was at a point in my life where my third eye had already received much healing because of the journey I had been travelling after my weight loss. I was open to those beliefs changing, which is such a crucial part of creating transformation of any kind in our lives. I feel so blessed to have travelled a path where this happened for me naturally. I feel that one of the biggest reasons for that is so that I could help others to navigate the path as well. My entire journey thus far is a perfect example of what happens when we take an extremely unbalanced brow chakra on a healing journey.

Back in 2010, I embarked on what was to be my final "weight loss" journey. During that initial phase of the journey, I was obsessively focused on the number on the scale. I allowed it to define me and I didn't care what I did to make it go down. Looking back on that time, I realised that some things I did to lose the weight back then were actually not healthy. Thankfully, along the way it turned into a weight "release" journey as I realised that I had much healing to do on the inner me in order that I could release the weight for ever. Finally, it turned into a health journey which has continued to this day and will continue for the rest of my life. I have learned so much along the path to finding a healthier me. Many of my deep-rooted beliefs have changed along the way and that couldn't have happened if my third eye was still majorly blocked or unbalanced.

This became very clear a few years ago when I had to do a business exercise. I was working on understanding the people I am trying to help more, so that I can help them in the best way for them. As part of that process, I had to put myself into the shoes of that person, which is usually easier for me than it may be for some people. It's easier when you've actually walked that path yourself, so I put myself back into the mind of 180 kilo Shari and started answering the questions. One question gave me one of the biggest "aha" moments of my life up to that point. It was, "What are your core life beliefs?" There were 3 lines there, so I automatically, without thinking, wrote 3 things:

1. Everything happens for a reason
2. Everyone is more important than me
3. I'm a bad person

I sat back and looked at what I had written and was absolutely gobsmacked. The first belief is something that I've always believed and probably always will. I'm ok with that being one of my core life beliefs as it works for me. It's functional in my life. It was the last 2 beliefs that were so revealing. I actually didn't realise that those two beliefs were in there. When you feel like that about yourself, why would you do anything good for yourself? Consciously we might try, but subconsciously we don't feel as if we deserve anything good in our lives, so eventually we will self sabotage and undo any progress we might have made, which is exactly what I had been doing for so many years. Having the belief that everyone else was more important than me also meant that I spent all of my time doing everything for everyone else and never did what I needed to do for myself. If I ever did do anything for myself, I felt so guilty! These beliefs also led to me continually looking outside of myself for validation and love. People pleasing was pretty much my whole life because it made me feel better about myself, if only for a little while. It was how I made myself feel needed, wanted, valued and important to people. Unfortunately, while I still held onto those beliefs, I was never going to like what I saw in the mirror either. Neither the mirror that reflected my physical body nor the inner reflection of my soul. Accordingly, I avoided both types of reflection as much as I could, including photos and videos. My daughter actually wrote me a letter when she was 9 or 10, begging me to let people take photos of me because one day she would need them to remember me by. It absolutely broke my heart to read that letter and as much as I loved her, I would still avoid having photos taken as much as possible.

What became clear to me when my old beliefs were revealed to me is that somewhere along my journey, those two beliefs changed. Thank goodness! I absolutely know, without a shadow of a doubt, that if they hadn't changed, then eventually I would have self sabotaged and gone back to 180 kilo Shari or possibly even worse. With the changing of those beliefs, a domino effect was started and my whole life has changed in so many positive ways. It has been like the unravelling of a big knotty ball of wool and with it has come the same sense of satisfaction and happiness as the knots come undone. There's still some unravelling to be done and that's ok. I'm healthy and happy now and with each knot released, I get a different perspective on that happiness.

Does my story resonate with you? Have you experienced some of these things yourself? Is there something in your life that you have been trying to change and you're struggling to do so? The next phase of your journey could require some healing and balancing of your brow chakra in order for you to finally break through. You never know what is going to be the first domino to fall and start the chain reaction. The first knot unravelled. The first thread pulled that keeps going until it's all undone. Consciously working on balancing your third eye chakra can only help you get to the next stage of your journey and I am so excited for you!

Below are some techniques or practices that can help you in your endeavours to balancing your third eye chakra. One of the biggest things I have learned on my journey is that there is no cookie cutter approach. There is no "one size fits all" to any of this. Different things work for different people and so it's important to try different things to see what works for YOU. When you look at the various healing techniques below, pick what resonates with you. There is no right or wrong. This is YOUR journey to unlocking your inner wisdom and reclaiming your inner goddess!

Sunlight

It is imperative for our health that we get adequate sunlight and it is also a powerful healing tool for our third eye. The element of the brow chakra is light and there are many benefits to getting out into sunlight daily and preferably in the morning sun. Ten minutes of beautiful sunlight on your skin in the morning will help to stimulate the pineal gland, improving the function of your brow chakra. It will have a positive impact on your health, your mood and will help to facilitate a clearer mind.

Blue/purple foods

As the colour of the sixth chakra is indigo (dark blue/purple), it is beneficial to be including foods of that colour into your daily nutrition. Fruits and vegetables which resonate with the brow chakra include: eggplant, blueberries, purple kale, prunes, raisins, dates, purple cabbage, figs, purple potatoes, blackberries and purple carrots.

Remove limiting beliefs

Our core beliefs drive our life, whether we realise it or not. If we have limiting beliefs such as "I'm a bad person", "I'm not important" or "I'm not good enough", we're definitely not going to feel connected to our inner wisdom. To connect with our higher selves, we must remove the limiting beliefs that are keeping us stuck in a place of insecurity, self-loathing and fear.

Being resilient in our thinking

To unblock our third eye, we have to have an open mind about exploring other viewpoints and perspectives. Being rigid and close-minded in our thinking is the total opposite of where we need to be to access the power of our inner knowing and reclaiming our inner goddess. Participating in activities out of our comfort zone, watching new shows or reading books can help us be more open-minded, as well as genuine curiosity about the ways of life and perspectives of those around us.

Keep a dream diary

We dream about what we need, fear or desire unconsciously, so by spending time reflecting, journaling, analysing and interpreting our dreams, we can uncover some deep-rooted issues that we may not be aware of. One of the brow chakra's responsibilities is to help us interpret our dreams and when we add this into our daily practice, it's amazing what insights we reveal to ourselves. The meanings of our dreams are individual to us and so the meaning that we find within them from our own reflection is what is most important.

Herbs

One of the most beneficial ways of administering herbs is to make a tea out of them. Alternatively, you can burn them like incense, diffuse them, apply a diluted form topically or consume them in various ways. Rosemary, jasmine, mugwort, blue lotus, lavender, basil, star anise, passionflower and saffron are wonderful for the brow chakra.

Self-reflection

When we reflect or analyse why we do what we do or how we think, we increase our levels of self-awareness. All change begins with awareness. This is key! It's a skill like anything else and by cultivating it and including it into our daily practice, we grow exponentially. A simple way to implement self reflection into our daily lives is to journal. Even just a few minutes of journaling each day around our thoughts, feelings, beliefs and behaviours can have massive benefit to not only our lives, but the lives of those around us.

Yoga

Yoga harmonises your energy and helps to balance your third eye chakra. Specifically, poses such as child's pose, janu sirsasana (head-to-knee pose), uttanasana (standing forward bend) and dolphin pose are great for the brow chakra.

Mindfulness

For optimised third eye function, it's important that we are grounded in reality. By focusing on being present in everything we do, we avoid getting lost in a world of delusion and fantasy. Focusing on conscious breathing can help with mindfulness a lot.

Visualisation

Take a couple of minutes to close your eyes and visualise a beautiful ball of indigo light emanating from your third eye chakra. Watch as the pulsating energy effortlessly erases all blockages and energises your entire body. We can add this to our daily practices to help keep our third eyes balanced and unblocked.

Pineal Gland decalcification

A blocked brow chakra can often be linked to the pineal gland, a tiny mass in the brain shaped like a pea which is responsible for the regulation of our reproduction hormones and sleep cycles. It's believed to be responsible for spiritual consciousness by ancient cultures including Chinese, Tibetan and Egyptian. Avoiding fluoride will aid in decalcifying the pineal gland.

Ask the Owl Spirit for guidance

The animal totem for the sixth chakra is the Owl. Ask Owl for guidance about what you need the most help with through visualisation, prayer, self-induced trance or meditation.

Candle Gazing

You can open your brow chakra by gazing into a candle flame. Place a candle at eye level in front of you and light it. Focus your gaze on the flame and stimulate the flow of energy within your body by practising mindful breathing at the same time.

Essential Oils

Diffusing oils or rubbing them on your wrist can assist with balancing the third eye chakra. Some good options include juniper, frankincense, sandalwood, vetiver, patchouli and clary sage.

Affirmations

Adding positive affirmations to your daily practice will help to keep your sixth chakra clear and balanced. Choose affirmations that resonate with you and that you truly believe. Some examples are "I look both inward and outward for wisdom", "I connect with the wisdom of the universe", "I have both clarity and peace of mind", "I create my reality", "I honour and trust in my intuition", "I am receiving and I am trusting", "I trust in myself", "I learn from my experiences".

Wear the colour indigo

Stimulate your sixth chakra by wearing indigo coloured clothing and accessories and by including the colour indigo in your surroundings.

Crystals

Certain crystals will help you balance your brow chakra. You can either carry them or meditate with them, choosing from crystals such as sodalite, kyanite, sapphire, amethyst, iolite, shungite, tanzanite, labradorite and lapis lazuli. As an example, sodalite amplifies intuition, while tanzanite helps with giving direction and healing.

"OM"

The sound that matches the vibration of the brow chakra is "OM". Humming or chanting the sound "OM" would be a wonderful addition to your daily practice to help keep your third eye chakra clear and balanced.

Binaural Beats

Listening to binaural beats can assist in clearing and activating all the chakras via alternating sound waves. Binaural beats is a form of music healing therapy.

Moon and star gazing

When we look into the expansiveness of the night sky, it certainly puts everything into perspective. By taking the time to go outside and stare at the moon and stars, you will open your mind up to different perspectives and thoughts you may not have considered previously.

As you can see, there are some very simple things that you can weave into your everyday life. Give yourself permission to start small and then layer from there. This is a journey and no matter which path you choose, you will arrive at your destination eventually. It's also important to point out that whilst we are working on balancing our third eye chakra, that we don't neglect the other chakras. There is no one chakra that is more important than any other and we must be careful that we don't unwittingly cause imbalance in the body by focusing only on the brow chakra. If you think of the chakras like a pyramid, what happens to the top of the pyramid if the lower levels aren't stable? It will all come crashing down, which is certainly not what we are trying to achieve by working on activating and balancing our third eye.

Finally, if, like me, you feel as if you may have created a dysfunctional physical or energetic suit of armour around yourself and are ready to remove it, then I have a special gift for you. I have created a very special process to do this that was channelled through my third eye in the middle of the night. Ajna would literally not allow me to sleep until it was channelled and documented in its entirety. The process helps you to remove the need for the dysfunctional physical or energetic suit of armour and to create a functional protective shield in its place. I have recorded it for you so that you may download it and listen to it whenever you need. You can access the recording here:

reclaimyourinnergoddess.com.au/resources

Before you move onto the next chapter, I want to remind you that you have absolutely everything you need inside of you. You have infinite wisdom and infinite power. The only limits you have are those that you place upon yourself. Who, but you, knows you the most intimately? Trust your inner voice. It knows all!

Resources:

To access the resources mentioned in this book go to
https://reclaimyourinnergoddess.com.au/resources

You Are the Bridge to The Cosmos-
Follow Your Life's Purpose Through the Crown

with Linda Joy Benn

*"Every woman who heals herself helps heal all the women who came before her,
and all those who come after her"*
– Christiane Northrup

You are an amazing soul. You chose to be here at this incredible time on the planet to experience and witness what is happening. Especially right now with a global pandemic. We are observing mass consciousness awakening. Remember who you are as a soul and how powerful you are. Keep your energy high, shine your light, and keep moving forward.

Advanced souls have karmically eventful lives. Many of us have experienced a traumatic past for our soul's evolution. On this journey, we have all agreed to go through these experiences for our soul's growth.

The reason I chose the crown chakra to write about is because it is known as "the bridge to the cosmos." It is the most spiritual of all seven chakras. It acts as your center for spirit, enlightenment, wisdom, universal consciousness, and connection to higher guidance. In a sense, the crown chakra is our highest potential. It governs interaction and communication with the universe. One's senses of inspiration and devotion, union with the higher self and the divine, and deeper understanding. It is also responsible for a healthy spiritual life of universal knowledge. It's like your umbilical cord to the divine, you are connected to the oneness of all things. Because of this direct connection, it is important that you do not conceptualize yourself as being separated from the divine. Instead, the greater universal force is merely a larger expansion of the same energy. Which you part of too.

You are the conduit between heaven and earth. Your crown chakra gives you the opportunity to remain connected to both. You are part of all that is. Energy flows through you like the infinity symbol, keeping you grounded and connected to the cosmos. Remain open and keep the energy flowing through your heart. The crossover point of the figure of 8 is at the heart center. This allows you to open your heart and let your love and light shine out to uplift others around you. Be kind and loving towards yourself, then share this positive energy with others.

By connecting to source via your crown, listen to your own internal GPS. You will automatically upgrade your conscious human operating system. Your brain can make clear choices and decisions for your highest good and destiny. This is a time of enormous growth and opportunity spiritually, mentally, and emotionally. When you drop into your heart, you will feel an increase in YOUR love that will expand out and attract more. DO LOVE, BE LOVE, and be the example for others to follow and radiate your love and light. When you surrender, practice letting go of control and attachments. You may experience yourself to receive more positivity, abundance, joy, peace, harmony, and happiness.

The Crown Chakra, in essence, guides you towards your destined path. Once you are content in knowing that there is a higher being looking out for you and supporting you in all that you do. You will let go of the fear, anxiety, and insecurities holding you back. A balanced crown chakra will help you make good decisions to move forward through spiritual guidance. You will be able to acknowledge your true power, and you will have no problems following through your life's purpose.

If you have health-related issues, pain in your body, anxiety, or fatigue. Or want clarity to solve problems, transform anger, grief, shame, guilt, sadness, hurt, and childhood trauma. These experiences cause energy blockages. Feeling out of balance, out of control, and having no direction in your life. I chose a healing career which helped me to heal and learn the skills to help others. I have experienced everything my clients come to me to resolve. This can be either emotional or karmic past experiences that is causing them pain. This led me to the formation of the 5R Renewal Program and the Benn Method™. I will share more about my Benn Method™ which is a compilation of over 20 years as a practitioner. Plus, my learnings from hundreds of teachers, mentors, and coaches. Over the last 30-plus years they have assisted in my healing from past trauma, karma, and helped me to understand what I agreed to learn in this lifetime.

There is a global problem of mental health. This includes depression, suicide, eating disorders, feeling unlovable, unworthy, not good enough, self-judgement, self-criticism, addictions, and self-destructive behaviours. Many people are going through challenging times. They feel pushed to the limits, stressed, overwhelmed, anxious, frustrated, or simply unhappy. This has led to relationship breakdowns.

I went through my own recovery. From cancer, chronic stress, adrenal burnout, chronic fatigue, autoimmune, suicide, depression, addictions and a 30-plus year eating disorder. Using my Benn Method and 5Rs, I transformed and restored my body to full health without medication or any medical intervention.

Look at everything you do in your life: the activities, decisions you make, how you interact with others. These affect your energy vibration. Your words, thoughts, emotions, and beliefs create your reality. In my programs, I help you upgrade your conscious human operating system. Imagine your brain is a computer. Using my methods is like going from an old computer operating system like DOS, which is limited and full of viruses, to installing a new "heart ware" system, which is conscious, aware and thriving.

This is why I created the BENN method. It is four profound steps to help open your heart to feel love and light. With every breath you will open your crown to connect with divine source.

BENN stands for

Balance, Energy, Nurture and Nourish = New Life/New YOU!

BENN METHOD™

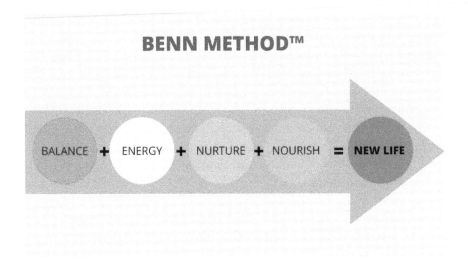

I can show you:

- How to work with energy pathways in your body even if you've never worked with energy before
- Why you must learn to accurately detect the flow of energy in your body
- What to do if you recognise energy blocks
- Multiple ways to redesign your internal energy flow to instantly boost your physical energy level, healing and joy
- How we influence our genes by our thinking and consciousness that can manifest disease in our body

Balance

Balance all areas of your life– physically, emotionally, mentally, energetically, and spiritually. Listen to your body. Your body is the barometer of the soul, guiding you to restore your health and wellbeing. When you ignore the body's signs or messages, it can lead to disease. Any imbalance in your work or life can lead to adrenal burn out, sleep imbalances, and illness. My prior lifestyle was totally imbalanced. I was always pushing myself with work, over exercise, lack of sleep, high cortisol and adrenal fatigue. I was saying yes when I meant NO, which led to my burnout.

When your life is out of balance, you are in survival mode. This is a stress response of fight or flight. This drains your energy of vitality, health, and in the long-term leads to disease. To move back into balance is to learn to self-regulate by being present and just breathe. When you breathe deeply down to your belly, it sends a message to the rest of your body via your nervous system that you are safe in your environment. By simply breathing and connecting to your heart. This shifts you out of your mind, which creates the illusion of stress, to a place of peace, harmony, and balance. When you're balanced, grounded, and focused, you can attract more abundance, love, joy, and health into your life.

The meditations I teach calm your mind and body, allowing you to remain relaxed, balanced, peaceful, and harmonious. Your goal is to deflect the lower energies that throw you off balance that cause stress, feeling burdened, and suffering. When you drop your focus into your heart, it opens you up to the joy of life.

In a state of balance, you will feel a connection with other beings, with the earth, with heaven, and with all the universe.

You will discover the seat of your wisdom, and you will get knowledge and integrate it with your life.

You will know and understand, and manifest divinity yourself.

A crown chakra that is not balanced or aligned will make you feel out of sorts. This includes feelings of indecisiveness, stress, fatigue, a sense of not belonging, anxiety, loneliness, meaninglessness, living in great fear or having little hope as you look forward to the future. If the crown chakra is blocked, all the other chakras, as well as your body and mind, will be affected.

The crown chakra is your connection to the spiritual world and your innermost self. There are many ways that you can cleanse, balance, and heal your crown chakra. In this chapter, I give you some tips to balance your crown chakra.

Energy

Energy- You are a powerful energy being connected to source energy. You can shift the energy, heal your body, and change the cells in your body by your intention and thought. Life force energy is flowing through you constantly. This allows you to remain high vibration, energetic, and live a joyful life with vitality.

When I cut off my connection from source, I saw my energy and physical body quickly deteriorated. This is why it's so important to connect to source through meditation and breathing. You can feel the flow of energy to heal your body. Now's the time to deepen your connection with source and upgrade your heart-ware. You can co-create everything you desire in your life.

Sleep is vital for your energy to make clear choices throughout the day. If you feel fatigued, ask your body what it needs, it could be as simple as taking a nap.

Nurture

Nurture is all about self-love, self-acceptance, self-worth, self-awareness, self-care, self-compassion, and self-forgiveness.
Nurturing your inner child and listening to your soul's calling.
Look at your shadow-self that requires healing and nurturing.
Do you see your body through the eyes of love?

This was a big learning moment for me when navigating out of an eating disorder. Give to yourself first, through self-care. Fill up your cup, be kind and loving to you! This can be as simple as taking a bath, saying NO to others, having a nap, or sitting quietly in a garden with a cup of tea.

When you tune into your heart, you can transform any reaction into a loving action. This will improve your overall health and wellbeing.

Nourish

Your mind and body. Make healthy food choices for your body. Read books to feed your mind and consciousness. Nourish your soul with meditation, healing techniques and personal development tools. Allow yourself to surrender and let go to accept what is. Always come back to the present moment and breathe. Fill yourself up with source energy. Focus on positive thoughts, people, and activities that make you feel good and that nourish your soul.

"Be the divine light that you are"

A higher power will guide you, and you will experience divinity from inside and out. The universal life force penetrates your energy system through the crown.

The challenge of the crown chakra is liberating the spirit and opening to the divine. At the same time staying firmly rooted to the ground. We can recognise signs of a polluted crown chakra in people who feel completely sure they are right. Especially the fanatical ones who force other people to comply.

The crown chakra is symbolised by a lotus with one thousand petals. With this sense of wholeness comes the feeling of an ending. The completion of a cycle, and the promise of something new. Elementally, it is associated with thought and silence, the mantra is, "I know." You will discover the seat of your wisdom, and you will get knowledge and integrate it with your life. You will simply know and understand, and you will manifest divinity yourself.

The crown chakra's sound is OM. The OM symbol is peace. Be peaceful, be loving and feel the peace within. Some illustrations of the crown chakra symbol include an "Om" image sitting in the lotus' centre. Because of this chakra's location, it is closely associated with the brain and the entire nervous system.

The energy of the crown chakra allows you to experience mystical oneness with everything and everyone. Plus, it gives you a sense of knowing that there is a bigger and deeper meaning in life. There is an order that governs all of existence with the collective pool of consciousness.

When you truly understand that everything is interconnected, and part of a larger scheme. You will also start living in gratitude, trust, and faith, instead of anxiety and fear. In essence, the crown chakra focuses on being of service to others. This includes your values and observing high ethics. Being a humanitarian and being sensitive to the environment.

The crown chakra allows for the experiences of unity and universal connectedness, as well as the integration of the whole. It has a masculine energy and is often represented by the colour violet. This is the colour of your connection with the energies of heaven. This colour also signifies rebirth and illumination. It connects with the sadness of letting go, as well as with the happiness of transformation.

The colour violet is also very cleansing and purifying. It's the colour of magic, mysticism, mystery, connection, purification, cleansing, and ritual. It's the colour that gives you a glimpse of other realities which are beyond your physical and material reality. It's the colour of reconciliation and brings together polarities.

On a physical level, violet is associated with the cerebral cortex, the brain, and the skull. It is primarily associated with the pituitary gland, and secondarily to the hypothalamus and the pineal. They work as a team to regulate the endocrine system. People who have developed their chakras experience the energies in their body flowing freely. From the bottom chakras all the way to the top chakras. They also radiate peace, health, and effortless energy. They also have good reflexes and respond to changes in their environment. A healthy crown chakra allows you to enjoy simple physical pleasures without becoming addicted to them.

On a mental level, the violet colour of this chakra is symbolic of being curious, open-minded, and a deep thinker. A developed crown chakra fosters a love for studying, reading, and learning. People with a strong crown chakra enjoy a healthy nervous system and a sharp mind. They possess excellent cognitive skills and overall physical health. When this chakra is strong and healthy, you will enjoy complete access to your subconscious and unconscious mind.

On an emotional level, this violet chakra fills you with the energy of completion or the end of a cycle. It's the colour of release, letting go, or making room for something new. Violet may contain deep sadness or grief. But it also comes with the acceptance of everything that happens on your journey in life. It's about suffering and hurting within the joy of living. Violet also resonates with being perceptive, sensitive, and intuitive. The emotional challenge is you may feel ungrounded or disconnected sometimes. You can feel overwhelmed or dissociated from your body. A developed crown chakra helps you to have wisdom and mastery and be aware of everything that's going on around you, detached from illusion. You will be immersed in joy, peace, and serenity.

With a developed crown chakra, you are spiritually and emotionally connected and balanced. Overall, you have a peaceful, calm, and joyful outlook, greatly influenced by knowing you are connected to heaven and grounded on earth. This chakra is the centre of your link with the universe, the infinite and your higher consciousness— it's the connection between wisdom and spiritual insight. With a developed crown chakra, you can give without the need for praise, recognition, or acknowledgment. When the energies are flowing freely to the crown chakra, you will be able to know the difference between your spirit-mind and your ego-mind. You will become more aware and freer. You will also be able to accept yourself for who you truly are. You can give from the place of your own inner completeness. Your oneness with the divine and your spiritual freedom allows you to be more intuitive, seeing the big picture, strengthening your psychic gifts and your ability to sense divine plans.

When the crown chakra is active, you'll feel the unity of everything and everyone in this world, deep and imaginative. What's important to you is being of service to others while strengthening your spirituality and achieving healing. The crown centre is the area where ethereal light and energy are received and then dispersed throughout your aura for total well-being. This allows for a sense of being connected to the body on a physical, emotional, mental, and spiritual level.

To balance this chakra, I find that meditation, breath work, yoga, spiritual healing, acupuncture, and colour therapy work best.

1. Meditate

Meditation will deeply influence your crown chakra because it's your connection to the higher power and to your higher self.

Visualize a golden light illuminating the crown of your head, including that space just above it. Feel this glow recharge and illuminate both your body and spirit.

Allow this soft but powerful light to reconnect you with the world, with your own authentic self, and with your own true light.

Regularly meditating is very beneficial. If you only have a few minutes to meditate, just try to imagine a violet lotus flower on top of your head for a simple but effective crown chakra meditation.

2. Leave your ego at the door

Ego and self-confidence are two entirely different things. Insecurity usually fuels ego. True confidence comes from acceptance and true knowledge of yourself.

Learning to release yourself from an ego-driven life will benefit you in so many ways.

3. Be compassionate and help others

Reaching out and helping others will strengthen your connection to your world, which is one of the crown chakra's main purpose.

4. Choose love

You can't fully love another person until you learn to love yourself. Loving yourself for who you truly are is the first step in accepting others.

When you choose to love each time, you are also letting go of tension present in your other chakras.

5. Pray

Prayer can be as simple as setting your intentions in your yoga practice. Just close your eyes and allow your deeper voice to be your guide. Pray to find your innermost self and to tap into the stillness that lies within you.

6. Yoga Asanas

Most yoga asanas are beneficial to the crown chakra because of their meditative aspect. Slow practice that allows time for lots of focus on the breath is very good. It is not striving to achieve challenging poses, but working on mindfulness and meditation.

7. Aromatherapy

Aromatherapy for the crown chakra includes a wide range of scents. You can use flowery essential oils, such as lavender, rose, and jasmine to soothe an overactive crown chakra.

More pungent essential oils such as myrrh, frankincense, and sandalwood can stimulate a blocked or underactive chakra.

8. Spend some time out in the sun

The crown chakra's elements are light and thought, so spending time under the sun is beneficial for unblocking or balancing the crown chakra.

Read books, solve crossword puzzles, or watch a thought-provoking documentary while sitting out in the sun. It's an easy way to heal this chakra.

9. Healing e.g. Reiki, Pellowah or other healings

A healing is a beautiful and loving way to bring balance to your crown chakra.

By using certain touch points on or around the body, the energy centres are cleared, re-structured and a new level of awareness is achieved. Pellowah healing is a shift in consciousness, connects 12 strands of DNA, expanding awareness. Though no touching, as it is more of an enlightenment modality. The healing is secondary when the consciousness has shifted.

As the crown chakra oversees and governs the functions of all chakras, using specific chakra stones will also heal the rest of the body. Healing can resolve particular health problems. Plus manage specific areas of the brain, the nervous system, the pineal gland, the pituitary gland, and all master glands. As the pituitary gland secretes hormones that align your whole system. It's important that you keep the crown chakra area healthy.

When activated, the Crown Chakra holds many gifts and blessings. This serves to improve a person's life and personality via a process of emotional healing.

In this process, you will experience a feeling of oneness with the people around you. United in humanity, you'll be drawn towards being more selfless and compassionate towards all others. Realizing that every little experience that life brings your way is actually part of a much larger scheme. You will be more grateful for all the people in your life and for all your experiences. This has been my realization through my healing journey. I will share my story soon.

Your past experiences have taught you some very valuable lessons to move you forward. Once realized, you will be able to start living the life you have envisioned for yourself.

It also ensures that your bond with the higher realm is strengthened. This ensures that you can receive the guidance that your guardian angels are sending your way. Connecting with spirit fills you with a sense of liberation and courage to do things and take risks that you never thought you could before, for fear of failing. The biggest failure in life is to not have taken any risks. Which is why activating your Crown Chakra will enable you to stop playing it safe and step out of your comfort zone to explore new things. You are an unlimited, multidimensional being. Trust in your guidance and take the step forward and this will inspire and encourage others around you. Share your blessings and be of service, knowing that you are helping to change the world. A healthy crown chakra will make you love life, and you will no longer fear death. Each day will be more colourful because you will always find that spark of joy!

When aligned, you will expand to a point where it's possible to access and tap into the deepest sources of wisdom.

For over 20 years working with clients, my focus for wellness is addressing the root cause of the problem. The symptoms are the end result usually from an emotional issue. By resolving the issue creates a space for deep healing work on all levels. Including the physical, emotional, and etheric bodies.

The Benn Method™ helps you go from trauma to thriving, resulting in freedom, love, peace, and joy. BENN = Balance, Energy, Nurture, and Nourish. The BENN Method™ assists you in returning to your true authentic self of empowerment. You have the power to heal your body and soul, leading to a place where you are free of suffering and at peace.

My method also incorporates the 5R Renewal program. A five-step process that includes the physical, emotional, mental, energetic, and spiritual. Along with the five elements of earth, wood, fire, metal, and water. The tools you learn align your mind, body and spirit. This empowers you to take charge of your health and wellbeing by self-healing your body.

The 5Rs stand for:
- Release
- Realign
- Restore
- Rebalance
- Re-energise

5R RENEWAL MODEL™

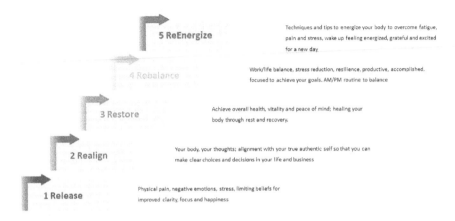

A little background about me, I was born in a small town on the east coast of Queensland, Australia. Born into a family that didn't understand me as we vibrate at different frequencies. I have learnt to accept and love them for who they are. As a soul, I came in as this bright light of joy but knew I was different from others. I was born with a natural intuitive gift, but I was trying to understand why my family didn't love or accept me. The more I shared my passions and purpose, the more I was ostracised. My life has been a journey to love and accept myself and not look outside for love or approval from others. My family members are playing important roles and I forgive them.

Now that I understand my birth chart, I have two planets in my 12th house. This explains why in this lifetime I share with humanity about the subconscious mind. We are all part of the collective consciousness. I channel profound messages from source or the universe through my crown chakra to share with others. Sharing this chapter on the crown which is connected to the collective consciousness. So you can remember who you truly are.

Though in my past I was carrying so much emotional pain of rejection, abandonment, and abuse. I was constantly asking why am I here? Why did I choose this family? Why am I being judged, criticised, and abused? I didn't like being in this body or living this life. Hence the eating disorder that started as a teenager. My older sister kept telling me that I was fat, ugly, and many other descriptive words. I created a belief that in order to be loved by anyone; I had to be thin, otherwise I would never get a boyfriend! I had depression growing up carrying so much emotional pain and suffering. Though on the outside I appeared happy to cover up the deep sorrow inside. I left home at 17 and moved to Brisbane to work. At 18, I received a letter from my mother telling me not to come home as I didn't have a home to come to. No one knew my story or the emotional pain I was carrying. To numb out, I would use food, drugs and alcohol to appear outgoing and a party animal. If anyone got too close to me, I would get scared to open my heart and be betrayed again. It was safer to shut down and run away and even leave the country. Hence, by age 30, I travelled all around the world to over 35 countries searching, wondering, where do I belong? Where is home and how do I love? Love was a painful word, as I had never experienced it. I realised my true home is in my heart. It's not where I physically live or who loves me. I am loved and supported by spirit. It has taken years of inner healing therapy to love and accept myself. Everything I have experienced over the years was all for a purpose—to help others. I have been blessed with amazing teachers over the years and many masters guiding me on my healing path.

At 21, I met my first spiritual teacher when I had cancer. I was backpacking around the world for three years and I met him in San Jose, California. For 6 months, I would go to his house every week. He helped me understand why I chose my family, what I was to learn, and my purpose for this life.

The turning point in my life was when I felt a calling to leave the corporate world and study natural medicine. This opened up a huge Pandora's Box, which I loved. I was like a sponge, absorbing as much as I could and my studies have continued. I started my holistic health business in 1999 in Australia, focusing on healing the mind-body connection. Some trainings include intuitive bodywork, remedial therapies, energy work, Reiki, Pellowah healing, facial harmony balancing, cranial sacral, Ortho-Bionomy, NLP, CBT-depression/trauma, Hypnotherapy, Time Line Therapy, Emotional

Freedom Technique, Yoga teaching, transformation coaching, trainer/assessor, psychic and tarot readings and many other modalities. A big "aha" moment I received was that you cannot heal the physical body with the mind that created it—the two work together. This realisation led me into teaching personal development workshops, coaching, and training to empower others to heal their own body. I believe we can change every cell in our body with our thoughts by what we focus on. I love sharing about epigenetics, neuroscience, quantum healing and how we are part of the collective.

In 2006, I travelled to the U.S. for a few months to teach Pellowah healing and share this powerful modality. Pellowah is a tool to help expand awareness and consciousness on the planet, which is in alignment with my purpose.

I relocated in 2010 to live in California for seven years. I felt I needed to return to my home country, as I could feel the political unrest happening. Plus, I was feeling exhausted, burnt-out, and needed to ground to recharge myself. When I contacted my family, the attacks and bullying started again. I fell into a dark depression and created a disease.

I stopped using my healing tools and everything I knew logically. Even though I knew my soul's purpose, I gave up my will to live. I closed down my crown chakra and cut off my connection to source energy and disconnected from my inner child, resulting in my physical body quickly deteriorating. I was committing energetic suicide. I take total responsibility for creating disease in my body; it was my way of escaping. Even though my soul knew why I came here as a lightworker.

I visited the dark side to experience where many people get stuck with depression, suicide, and illness. I had to go through it myself in order to relate and have compassion for others. I had everything stripped away so I could restructure my life. My body was in chronic stress causing an autoimmune disease, my thyroid is now balanced and normal.

Every organ and system was barely functioning. My liver was at 38%, my left eye was at 30%, I couldn't drive or focus. Now both eyes are great and I don't need glasses for long or short distances. This proves that we can heal every part of our body.

My brain could not concentrate or remember things. I was so fatigued; I had to keep having naps during the day. My adrenal test showed I had phase three adrenal fatigue; it was a flat line on the graph. I had massive sleeping issues as my nervous system was constantly in a stress response. Now I sleep soundly, have rebalanced my adrenals, and have my energy and mojo back.

To support you on your journey to vibrant health, I encourage you to commit to a 33-day habit to rewire your brain to accelerate results in your life. See below for the link.

Repeat this mantra to say, "All my needs are met for my physical, emotional and spiritual body." I surrender, I release, I let go…

With this mantra, you will begin to experience more of what you desire, while peace and gratitude will flow freely into your space. By embracing that gratitude, you welcome more powerful energy to help create your desires.

YOU are here to vibrate your light—let it shine!

Life is about freedom. We are all here to experience the freedom and love within us.

Mantra to repeat through the day—*I feel so blessed to be alive today.*

Oracle card message - Can you feel me?

Your feminine aspect is awakening. Feel the goddess energy inside you. She seeks acknowledgement and validation. New and wonderful things are coming into your life. Wake up! Celebrate.

You'll Achieve Spiritual Balance, Growth, and Expansion

You'll open up to a sense of something bigger, something infinitely powerful - that incredible spiritual aspect of ourselves. You'll awaken to the energies of higher purpose as you connect with your intuition to direct and guide you along the path that is right and true for you. You'll have the tools to overcome daily challenges and obstacles as you discover a deeper meaning to your existence - who you truly are and what you are meant to do in the world.

My whole journey has been about trusting the guidance direct from spirit. Learning to love, trust and have faith and an inner knowing that I will get through this.

Albert Einstein – "Few are those who see with their own eyes and feel with their own hearts"

So start feeling with your heart.

We learn to self-correct on our journey. Lead with your heart. Out of balance? Feel the emotions- feelings are inner knowing. Make decisions from your heart. Articulate the messages.

When we balance our chakras. When our crown chakra is shining with violet light, perfect like a lotus. We will then feel energy throughout our bodies, minds, emotions and spirits. Its important that we nurture and nourish ourselves as spiritual beings. We then feel the connection to each other and to divinity. When we have this deep knowing, we reclaim our inner goddess with joy, serenity, love and purpose.

I would love to support you on this journey called life. Please feel free to contact me and make sure to tap into the following gifts on our site resources: meditation, free consultation, and the 33 Day Challenge Guide at https://reclaimyourinnergoddess.com.au/resources

"A woman who walks in purpose doesn't have to chase people or opportunities. Her light causes people and opportunities to pursue her."

Resources:

To access the resources mentioned in this book go to
https://reclaimyourinnergoddess.com.au/resources

The End of the Adventure?

"The image of the Goddess inspires women to see ourselves as divine, our bodies as sacred, the changing phases of our lives as holy, our aggression as healthy, our anger as purifying, and our power to nurture and create, but also to limit and destroy when necessary, as the very force that sustains all life. Through the Goddess we can discover our strength, enlighten our minds, own our bodies, and celebrate our emotions. We can move beyond narrow, constricting roles and become whole."

– Starhawk

Congratulations! You have made it to the end of this adventure towards reclaiming your inner goddess. It may be the end of the book, but the start of a wild and liberating journey. When we align our chakras, we can live in flow.

When we started writing our chapters, we all soon discovered that we were working on the chakra we most needed to at the time. As a reader, you may have noticed that there were chakras you resisted or liked most. Life will often pull you out of alignment, but by being curious and open, it is possible to see where you are out of alignment in your chakras. You are welcome to dip back in to any chapter and chakra at any time as you need it. We are here within each chapter but we are also available in our online communities you are welcome to join.

So, what's next? Well, that our goddess friend is completely up to you! Our businesses and offerings are diverse and powerful and we welcome you to connect. We wrote this book as our offering in our world, to be of service, to make a difference and to give you the tools and inspiration to reclaim your inner goddess.

It seems fitting that we end with more wisdom from the author Starhawk:

"The long sleep of Mother Goddess is ended. May She awaken in each of our hearts - Merry meet, merry part, and blessed be."

Resources

To access the resources mentioned in this book go to
https://reclaimyourinnergoddess.com.au/resources

Lightning Source UK Ltd.
Milton Keynes UK
UKHW011014070223
416609UK00006B/1508